WHY YOU DON'T MESS WITH TEXAS

How the Battle of the Alamo and the Mexican-American War Forever Changed America

SANDRA ZINK, Ph.D.

BANYAN · TREE · PRESS

Why You Don't Mess With Texas: How the Battle of the Alamo and the Mexican-American War Forever Changed America

ISBN: 978-1-948261-19-7

Library of Congress Control Number: 2019907373

Cover Design and Interior Layout: Ronda Taylor, www.heartworkpublishing.com

Cover Image Credit: Courtesy of Texas State Library and Archives Commission, image 1/008-3, San Antonio. [Siege of the Alamo, March 6, 1836]. Photo of painting by L. R. Bromley, 1884.

BANYAN · TREE · PRESS

Denver, Colorado
Austin, Texas
www.BanyanTreePress.com

PRAISE FOR *Why You Don't Mess with Texas ...*

From Ruth McDonald, long-time resident of Loveland, now retired, who has developed an interest in American history to share with her grandchildren.

> "Sandra Zink has a way of summing up a story in an accurate and entertaining way. It wasn't hard to read or more complicated than it needed to be. Our historical figures, whose names have come down to us through time, feel very human and familiar. The personal stories of those men at the Alamo made them more real and their destiny more personal to the reader. I loved the maps and the boxes with little interesting tidbits to thread through the story, such as the Marine Hymn reference and significance of the red line on the blue uniform. I was particularly pleased to learn something of Mexico's political history—this is a country right next to us and I've never bothered to find out anything about its history or government. How different things would be today if México had had the means to defend that huge expanse of country back in the 1800's."

From Dave Richards, Semi-retired Construction Manager

> "I haven't spent a lot of time studying history. But I found this account of the Texas Revolution and the Mexican-American War very interesting and informative. I knew about the Battle of the Alamo from stories and movies, but I don't recall the Mexican-American War ever being taught to me in much detail as a young student. I think that the tendency was to portray the United States as the hero in American History (the pilgrims, founding fathers, revolutionary war, pioneers, WWI, WWII etc.). Sandra Zink's book is an unbiased account of this period in our history. Through reading this book, I have come to understand that while there were certainly heroic individuals that emerged from the war, there is also the reality that for the most part, the United States was the aggressor in this conflict."

DEDICATION

Dedicated to my son Wade Moody,
who initiated this journey of writing about our American history,

to Loki Holmes, who read my first beginning chapters
that described the Texas Revolution and the Battle of the Alamo,

and to my son Allen Moody,
who encouraged me to complete the journey by creating this book.

CONTENTS

—CHAPTER ONE—

—CHAPTER TWO—

—CHAPTER THREE—

PREFACE

This book began as an introduction to Texas and the Battle of the Alamo for my great-grandson when we were planning a visit there in 2016. He was ten years old. But as I began to do my research about the history of Texas, I realized how little I knew about the Texas Revolution and the Mexican-American War that followed.

My exposure to the Battle of the Alamo, as portrayed in books and movies, described our heroic western frontiersmen, such as Davy Crockett, dying at the hands of a brutal dictator who led an army of thousands to defeat a few hardy men in Texas. But there was so much more to the story of the birth of the Republic of Texas and how Texas became a state.

The Mexican-American War that followed placed a new boundary between the United States and Mexico and created profound changes in both countries. America now crossed the continent to the Pacific Ocean. The capture of California fueled a dynamic economic engine for the United States.

But the addition of new western land for settlement opened the wound of potential expansion of slavery into new territories. It would require the American Civil War to force the end of slavery forever.

Mexico would endure long periods of conflict as it sought to realize a stable government free of dictatorships. Its own civil wars would occupy the country until 1920 when a stable constitutional republic was established.

With the encouragement of my family, I realized that a book written as an abbreviated history might appeal to a young reader in the middle-school to high-school age and perhaps enlighten the older reader as well. I have attempted to present a factual account of events so that the reader can understand how and why they occurred. A text-book style of presentation was used to make it easier to search for particular sections.

Many of the young soldiers in the Mexican-American War became famous generals in the American Civil War thirteen years in the future. A young lieutenant, Ulysses S. Grant, would become General-in-Chief of the Union North armies in the Civil War and bring the war to its final conclusion. Robert E. Lee, a brilliant army engineer in the Mexican-American War, became General-in-Chief for the Confederate South. Grant and Lee would face each other as enemies in the final battles of the war. Lee surrendered to Grant at Appomattox.

I have tried to show how this part of history of America and Mexico had lasting consequences and shaped the future of both countries. It is my hope that it can contribute to a more informed understanding of America's past.

AN OVERVIEW

Without the Texas Revolution and the Mexican-American War, California, Texas and the Great Southwest would not be part of the United States; they would belong to Mexico. The border wall between the two countries would stretch from near New Orleans on the Gulf Coast, across the Southwest and the Great Basin of Nevada and Utah, to the Oregon border, before heading west to the Pacific Ocean. The great prize of California, with an economy today that ranks fifth in the world, would still be part of Mexico.

When the Texans fought for their independence from Mexico, the Texas Revolution was the first step of a massive expansion of the United States. The Mexican-American War would occur less than a decade later and yield a huge area of land for American settlers. These two events transformed the American landscape, but also sowed the seeds for the American Civil War thirteen years in the future, a four-year conflict that would cost hundreds of thousands of lives, end slavery and cement the country as a "United" States of America.

The Texas Revolution began in 1835 when Mexican President Antonio Lopez de Santa Anna attempted to confiscate a cannon from the militia of the Texas colonists at Gonzales, Mexico, and the Texans refused. Their resistance quickly grew into a major conflict when Santa Anna brought a large army to face down the rebelling Texans at the Alamo.

The Battle of the Alamo in 1836 became a lasting symbol of heroic self-sacrifice as a few hardy men faced Santa Anna's army of thousands and died for the liberty of Texans. Their dedication to the cause became a rallying cry for a new Texas army, which defeated Santa Anna in the Battle of San Jacinto, April 21, 1836, and created the Republic of Texas, an independent nation for almost ten years.

The annexation of Texas in December 1845 as the 28th state of the Union quickly escalated tensions between the two countries since Mexico did not recognize the Texas boundaries that had been defined after Santa Anna's defeat in 1836.

Ignoring the rising friction, American President James K. Polk in 1846 was determined to expand America across the entire North American continent from the Atlantic to the Pacific Ocean. It was America's "destiny." To gain Mexico's Territories of Alta California and Nuevo (New) Mexico, Polk soon initiated the Mexican-American War by sending troops into the disputed land claimed by both Mexico and Texas.

The professional army of the United States led by two capable generals, Zachary Taylor and Winfield Scott, defeated the Mexican armies in a series of battles in Mexico over the next two years. The war ended in September 1847 with the surrender of the capital of Mexico City.

The weak and disorganized Mexican military in California had been defeated some months earlier by the U.S. Navy and a coalition of U.S. army and navy forces located there. Mexico's Territory of Nuevo Mexico was claimed by the U.S. Army between August 1846 and March 1847 with the capture of Santa Fe, New Mexico, and the defeat of Mexican forces in Chihuahua, Mexico.

In the treaty of 1848, Mexico was forced to cede half its lands to the United States. The new territory granted all the disputed land claimed by the Republic of Texas, plus what would become California, Arizona, Nevada, New Mexico, and parts of Colorado, Utah and Wyoming. The United States was now an unbroken expanse of land across the continent, adding territory as large as that acquired in the Louisiana Purchase.

But the massive land grab brought to the surface the country's divisiveness over the issue of slavery. Vast new territories were now available for settlement and wealthy southern slaveholders, who had attained great power in national politics, were advocating slavery in the territories to support new cotton plantations. Cotton was a major export for the United States in 1850, providing more than two-thirds of the world's supply.

Slavery would divide the country, North and South, for the next decade. Antislavery advocates demanded no expansion of slavery in the new lands, while proslavery forces insisted that the new territories had the Constitutional right to make their own decision. Heated discussions in the Houses of Congress and the country at large debated the issue.

The Compromise of 1850 brought an uneasy calm by granting California statehood as a free state, but allowed the territories of Utah and Arizona to self-determine their slavery status. The Kansas-Nebraska Act of 1854 nullified the Missouri Compromise of 1820 which had excluded slavery north of Missouri's southern border, except in Missouri itself.

With the election of President Abraham Lincoln in 1860, his rejection of slavery in the new territories set the stage for Southern secession, initiated by South Carolina in December 1860.

Within a few weeks, ten more states, including Texas, had joined South Carolina in seceding from the Union. The American Civil War was launched April 12, 1861, when the Confederate States of America fired on Fort Sumter, a United States garrison, in Charleston, South Carolina.

The four-year struggle would take the lives of more than 620,000 American soldiers and uncounted thousands of civilians. Many young men fighting together as fellow soldiers in the Mexican-American War of 1846-48 became seasoned generals for the Confederate South and the Union North, and faced each other as enemies in battle.

When the Civil War concluded May 9, 1865, the Union remained intact and slavery was ended. The 13th Amendment abolishing slavery and involuntary servitude was passed by the U.S. Senate in April 1864 and by the House of Representatives on January 31, 1865. It was ratified by the required number of states in December the same year.

Mexico faced a challenging future after its losses in the Mexican-American War. A weak economy and a disorganized government prompted competing political factions to alternately seize and lose power for several decades. The Conservatives, a coalition of the Catholic Church and the military, battled against the Liberals, who advocated religious tolerance and economic measures that would enable rural indigenous populations of the country to become full citizens. It was not until after Mexico's Civil War, also known as the Mexican Revolution, between 1910 and 1920, that Mexico achieved a constitutional republic, ending a long history of dictatorships.

CHAPTER ONE

THE TEXAS REVOLUTION

1.1 INTRODUCTION AND TIMELINE

When Mexico achieved independence from Spain in 1821, the northern region of its territory that bordered the United States was sparsely populated. The few hardy settlers who had migrated into the area were frequently subjected to raids from Comanches, the foremost Native American tribes in the Southwest. Abandoned homes and ranches prompted the Mexican government to encourage immigration of new settlers into the region by offering free land to help combat the frequent raids. Thousands of Americans responded.

Within ten years, a large population of Anglo-American immigrants occupied a region around San Felipe, a town on the Brazos River, in the Mexican state of Coahuila y Tejas. As the number of immigrants increased, they expressed a growing resentment of the government's restrictions and laws that affected their lives. Mexican law, at times, contradicted some of America's Bill of Rights and the U.S. Constitution that the new immigrants had learned to expect, such as freedom of religion.

Tensions continued to grow as Mexico's newly elected President Antonio Lopez de Santa Anna invoked new laws in 1835 that increased taxes and implemented a centralist government which removed many of the rights and privileges of the state governments. State militias were eliminated. When Santa Anna attempted to confiscate the cannons that had been distributed to settlers as protection against the Comanches, the Anglo-American settlers at Gonzales, about ninety miles from San Felipe, resisted and refused the demand. The brief skirmish in October 1835 resulted in the first shots of the Texas Revolution.

The conflict at Gonzales was quickly followed by the Siege of San Antonio, the Battle of the Alamo, flight of the settlers from the pursuing Mexican army, and the final battle at San Jacinto, which the Texans won. The capture of Santa Anna resulted in the Treaties of Velasco, which granted Texas the lands north of the Rio Grande and gave birth to the Republic of Texas. Admission of Texas as a state to the United States ten years later set the stage for the Mexican-American War.

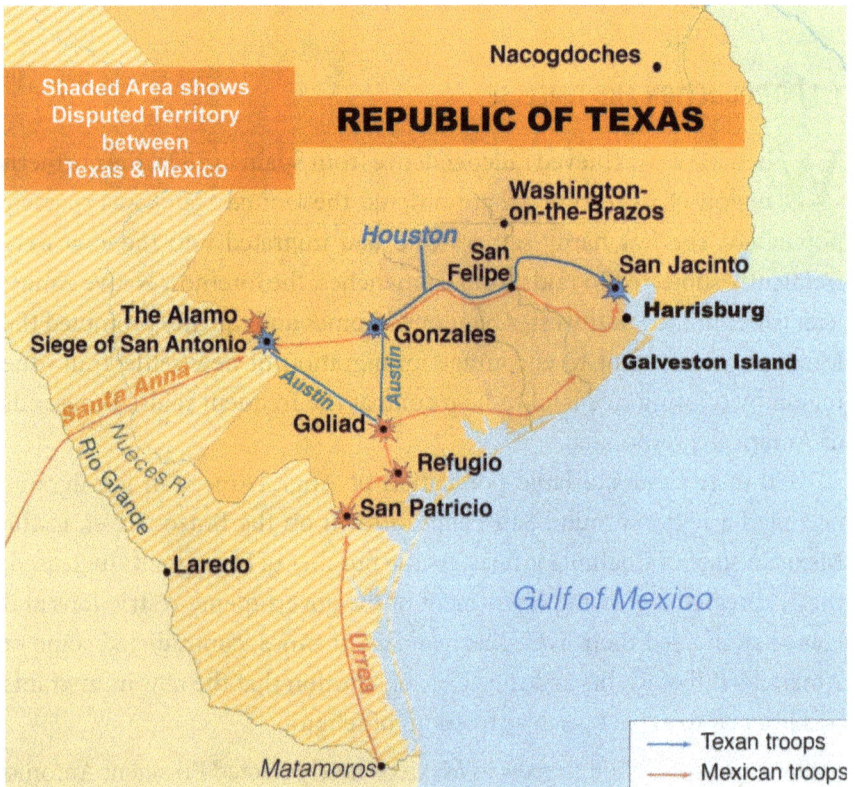

Texan and Mexican troop movements during Texas Revolution 1835-36.
Map Credit: Mapping Specialists, Ltd., Fitchburg, WI, modified by Sandra Zink

TIMELINE OF TEXAS REVOLUTION

1822–1828: Stephen Austin leads first Anglo-American settlements to immigrate to Mexico, settling at San Felipe on the Brazos River in Coahuila y Tejas, the northeastern state of Mexico.

1822–1834: Large numbers of Anglo-American immigrants, now called Texians, soon outnumber the native-born Mexicans.

1834–1835: New President Antonio Lopez de Santa Anna invokes the Mexican Constitution of 1835 that reduces the independence of state and local governments, eliminates their militias and then imprisons Stephen Austin when he proposes a separate Mexican state of Texas.

October 2, 1835: Battle of Gonzales. First shots of the Texas Revolution. Texian colonists resist Mexican demands to give up their cannon.

November 1–December 9, 1835: Texians invoke Siege of San Antonio and capture The Alamo from Mexican troops.

November 7, 1835: Texas Consultation meets at San Felipe de Austin and creates a new Texas Army, headed by Sam Houston.

February 23–March 5, 1836: Mexican Army, headed by President Santa Anna, arrives at the Alamo and initiates a siege against the Texans.

March 2, 1836: Texas Declaration of Independence declares the birth of the Republic of Texas at Washington-on-the-Brazos; delegates write a new Constitution.

March 6, 1836: Battle of The Alamo. Santa Anna orders all Texas defenders killed or executed.

March 11, 1836: The "Runaway Scrape." Texans flee the pursuing Mexican Army.

March 27, 1836: Goliad Massacre: more than 400 prisoners executed.

April 21, 1836: Battle of San Jacinto; Texas Army defeats Santa Anna and holds him prisoner.

May 14, 1836: Treaties of Velasco, signed by Mexican President Santa Anna, grant independence to the Republic of Texas.

October 1836: Houston elected first president of Republic of Texas.

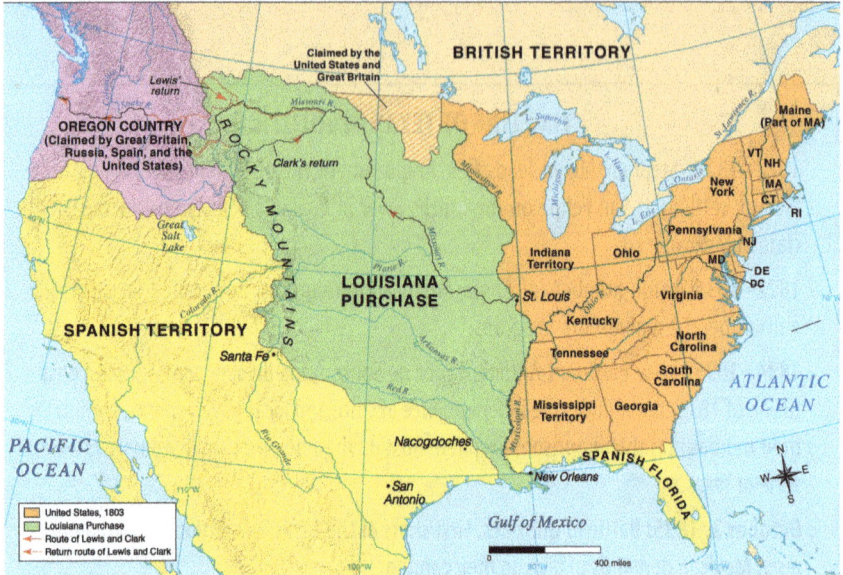

North America at time of Louisiana Purchase (1803)

Map Credit, Mapping Specialists, Ltd., Fitchburg, WI, modified by Sandra Zink

1.2 BACKGROUND LEADING TO TEXAS REVOLUTION

In 1803, the United States paid the government of France $15 million for the Louisiana Purchase, a vast territory of 827,000 square miles, which bordered Mexico, still under Spanish rule. Doubling the size of America, settlers and new immigrants soon moved westward into Louisiana Territory, and beyond.

Thousands crossed the Rocky Mountains into Oregon Country and many more into Spanish territories in California and the Gulf Coast near New Orleans. The coastal region was known as Spanish Tejas, pronounced "TAY-hass," a word meaning "friends" or "allies," from the Caddo people, who had occupied the region for over a thousand years before the arrival of the new settlers.

■ MEXICO ACHIEVES INDEPENDENCE FROM SPAIN

Mexico had been conquered in the 16th century by the Spanish Conquistador Hernando Cortes, who defeated the powerful Aztec empire. For the next three hundred years, the Spanish colonial government enforced great privileges for the Spaniards and oppressed the indigenous people, subjugating them to heavy taxes and brutal punishing laws. Out of this, several

4

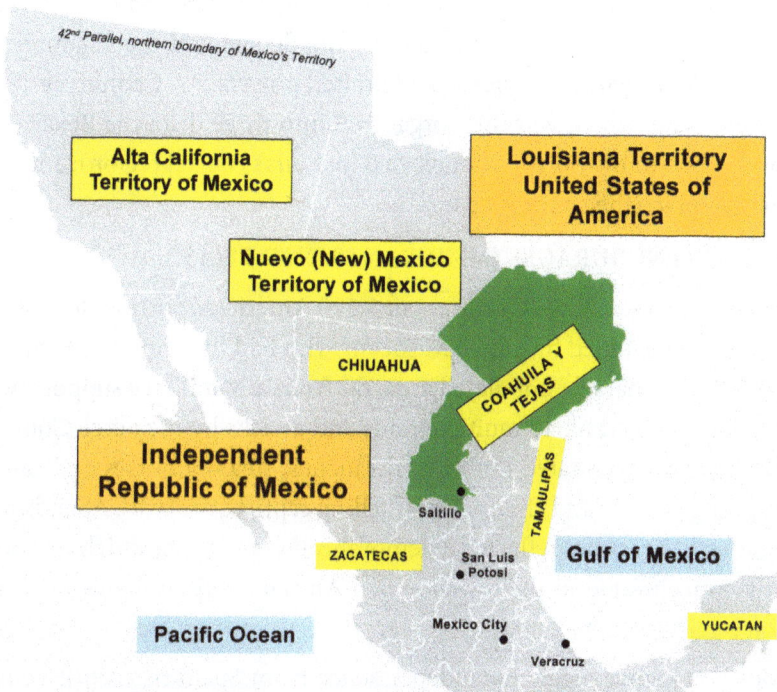

Status of Mexico after winning its independence from Spain
Map Credit: Wikimedia Commons, modified by Sandra Zink
For the names of all states, see: https://en.wikipedia.org/wiki/1824_Constitution_of_Mexico.

social classes were created, with the white colonists of pure Spanish blood at the top and the Indian peasant at the lowly bottom.

By 1810, native-born Mexicans, long suppressed by Spanish rule, were ready for independence and began a rebellion that would last eleven years, beginning with the famous "Cry of Dolores," when Priest Father Hidalgo of Delores, Mexico, rang the bell of his church, announcing the Call to Arms. The loose collection of peasants, farmers and Mexican-born Spaniards carried out guerilla warfare against their colonial masters for the next decade. Spain's battles with France and its own civil war finally tipped the balance in 1821 in favor of Mexico, which celebrates its independence each September 16, by ringing the same bell Father Hidalgo used in 1810.

"Spanish Tejas" became "Mexican Tejas," and in 1824 the now independent Mexico set up a federal republic of nineteen United Mexican States and four territories, plus a district around its capital, Mexico City. The nation's official religion was that of the Roman Catholic Church and protected by law. Legislative power was controlled by the Senate and the Chamber of Deputies. An executive president had limited powers.   Coahuila y Tejas became a state, which was then organized into three districts: Bexar (the Texas portion in the north); Monclova (Coahuila's central region); and Rio Grande Saltillo (the southern part).

■ MEXICO ENCOURAGES IMMIGRANTS INTO TEJAS

In 1821, Tejas contained only about 3,500 American-born settlers, sharing territory occupied by native Mexicans who had lived in the region for centuries. The sparsely populated area, far from any military support, was particularly vulnerable to multiple raids and attacks by the fierce Comanche tribes who decimated homes and ranches, stealing horses and cattle, kidnapping women and children, and selling captives as slaves. Abandoned haciendas and ranches reflected a demoralized population, which was now mostly concentrated in the towns of San Antonio and La Bahia, near the military garrison at Goliad.

Mexico's long struggle for independence from Spain had left it with a weak economy and an ineffective military, composed largely of peasants, conscripted native Indians and the few surviving professional soldiers from the war of independence. A further disadvantage was the great distance between the center of Mexico's national government at Mexico City and the northeastern regions of Mexico, limiting government support for Tejas, military or otherwise.

By encouraging immigration, the new government hoped to improve its local defenses against the raids and attacks by the Comanche and form stable communities. Following an established policy under Spanish rule, large land grants were provided to individuals in exchange for bringing in new settlers who would establish ranches and farms. The organizer or *empresario* would provide leadership to the settlers, interface with Mexican officials, and guide the settlement to success. Mexico approved twenty-four such grants, most of which were awarded to U.S. born natives.

■ THE AUSTIN LAND GRANT

One of the first Mexican land grants awarded to an American *empresario* was to Moses Austin from Missouri. Austin, born in Connecticut in 1761,

STEPHEN F. AUSTIN

Described as the father of modern Texas, Stephen Austin accompanied his parents around 1800 to what would become southeastern Missouri in 1820. Young Austin assisted his father, Moses, in the lead mining business as a young man. When the mining business failed, Moses was able to obtain a Spanish land grant in 1820 to settle families in northern Tejas, still under Spanish rule. Before the grant could be implemented, however, Moses died of pneumonia and his son, Stephen, took charge as the grant's empressario.

In 1821, Stephen obtained permission from the new independent government of Mexico to settle three hundred families on the Brazos River in Mexican Tejas. They became known as the "Old Three Hundred." Austin was a successful leader for the colony and secured additional grants in 1825, 1827 and 1828 to settle nine hundred more families in the colony, now known as Texians.

The political climate began to change around 1830 as the government gravitated to more centralist policies that placed increased taxes on the colonists, removed many of the states' rights that had been guaranteed in the 1824 Constitution and eliminated local militias.

When Mexican cavalry arrived at Gonzales in October 1835 to confiscate a cannon that belonged to the local militia, the colonists refused. In the confrontation, two Mexican soldiers were killed. Texians responded to the threat by forming a volunteer "Army of the People," with Austin serving briefly as its commander.

As tensions escalated, colonists rallied to create a Provisional Government, with its own Army of Texas, headed by Sam Houston. Mexican President Antonio Lopez de Santa Anna, determined to crush the Texas revolt, attacked the rebels at the Battle of the Alamo. All Texas defenders were killed. Additionally, more than four hundred prisoners were executed at the Goliad Massacre under Santa Anna's order of "No Quarter." Shortly afterward, the Texas Army under Sam Houston defeated Santa Anna at the Battle of San Jacinto and the Republic of Texas was born.

The new Texas Republic elected Houston as its first President in 1836 and Stephen Austin was named Secretary of State, but died of pneumonia after only two months in office.

married into an affluent mining family in Virginia. He and his brother implemented a successful lead mining business in Wythe County, Virginia, in the 1790s. Although initially successful, the business failed around 1796 and Moses soon moved with his family to a rich lead mining region in upper Spanish Louisiana, not far from the Mexican border. His good fortune continued when the Louisiana Purchase in 1803 brought him and his mining operation into the United States.

Moses Austin became a successful businessman, building a mine, smelter and a town, until the Panic of 1819 left him bankrupt. Aware that the Mexican government was encouraging immigration into Mexican Tejas, Austin traveled to San Antonio in 1820 and got approval for a land grant to settle three hundred families in the northern half of Tejas.

Before he could implement the plan, however, Moses died of pneumonia in 1821 and left the land grant to his son, Stephen F. Austin, who went forward with the colonization plan. The first group of colonists, known as the "Old Three Hundred," arrived in 1822 and settled at San Felipe de Austin in a coastal plain near the Brazos River. Austin was an effective leader, creating civil and criminal codes, distributing land to the colonists, campaigning against threats from the Comanche Indians, while maintaining good relations with the Mexican authorities. With this early success, Austin was able to obtain additional land grants in 1825, 1827 and 1828 to settle nine hundred more families.

> ## TEXAS RANGERS
>
> In 1823, Stephen Austin created the Committee of Public Safety and hired ten tough and experienced frontiersmen for $15 a month to protect his colony of immigrants from the Comanche and other Native American tribes. Formally constituted as Texas Rangers in 1835, they played an active role as a paramilitary force in Texas' history and continue to be legendary in law enforcement today. Many participated in the Mexican-American War, and their tactics in the Battle of Monterrey earned them the name "Texas Devils" from the Mexican soldiers. Their heroic history has been documented in scores of books and plays and established them as a significant icon in the mythology of the Wild West. A well-known fictional character of the West, The Lone Ranger, derives his name from the Texas Rangers.

The Mexican government encouraged the colonists to create their own militias to defend against the raiding Comanche Indians and enforce the local and federal laws. Some weapons and a few cannons were distributed to the new colonists. With no army to protect them, Austin created the Committee of Public Safety which would later become the famous Texas Rangers, tough men skilled in frontier warfare. The Rangers defended settlers from the Comanches, earned fame in the Mexican-American War for

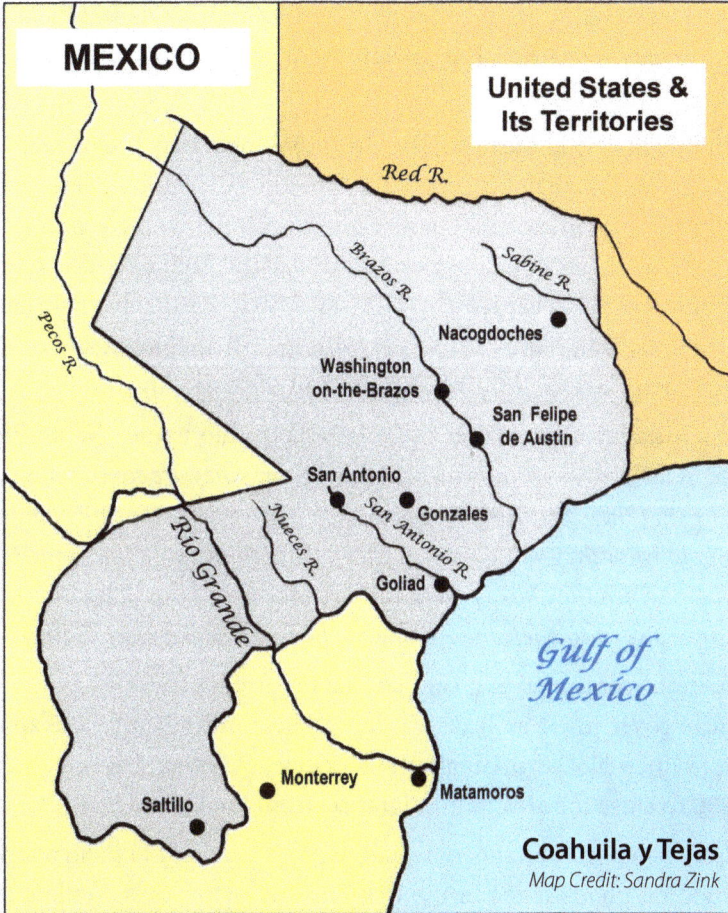

MEXICO

United States & Its Territories

Red R.

Brazos R.

Sabine R.

Pecos R.

Nacogdoches

Washington on-the-Brazos

San Felipe de Austin

San Antonio

Gonzales

San Antonio R.

Nueces R.

Rio Grande

Goliad

Gulf of Mexico

Monterrey

Matamoros

Saltillo

Coahuila y Tejas

Map Credit: Sandra Zink

their fighting ability, and eventually subdued the threat from the Indians, defeating them in several battles in the 1840s.

■ MEXICO CLOSES ITS IMMIGRATION POLICY

The population of immigrants continued to grow in Tejas as more *empresarios* brought new colonists into the region. Many of them were farmers from nearby cotton states and brought their slaves with them. In 1830, estimates placed the Anglo population at 20,000, plus about 1,000 slaves, compared to 5,000 Mexicans.

The Anglo-American immigrants in Mexican Texas, known as Texians, now outnumbered the native population (Tejanos) four to one. In Nacogdoches, near the Louisiana border, the ratio of Texians to natives was greater at ten to one. Although the new immigrants were required to pledge loyalty to Mexico, learn Spanish and convert to Catholicism, many ignored their pledges.

Unfamiliar with Mexican law, they assumed that the United States' Constitution, less than fifty years old, was still valid, guaranteeing freedom of religion as a fundamental basic right, in conflict with Mexican law that declared the only allowed religion was that of the Roman Catholic Church. Settlers largely disregarded the Mexican restrictions, kept their language and cultures, maintained strong ties with the United States, and continued to keep their slaves in spite of Mexico's ban of slavery in 1829.

The Mexican commander of La Bahia presidio wrote *"No faith can be placed in the Anglo—American colonists because they are continually demonstrating that they absolutely refuse to be subordinate, unless they find it convenient to what they want anyway...they do nothing more than practice their own laws which they have practiced since they were born, forgetting the ones they have sworn to obey, these being the laws of our Supreme Government."*

Tensions continued to grow between the American immigrants and the Mexican government as Texas was rapidly beginning to appear as an American province. Not surprisingly, the Mexican government enacted new laws in 1830 to close the area to immigration from the United States.

Established immigrants now had to pay a property tax and a tariff was imposed on goods made in the U.S. Further, many Texas settlers refused to comply with Mexico's 1829 prohibition against slavery, so they forced their slaves (now numbering about 5,000) to become indentured servants. Immigration continued, but now illegally. By 1835, the number of Anglo-Americans had increased to 35,000, with 8,000 slaves.

Resistance grew as immigrants advocated for more independence. A group of Texians forced the Mexican garrison to leave Nacogdoches in August 1832 in a revolt against the government's military rule. Tensions continued to escalate as settlers demanded greater representation in the Mexican government.

■ TEXIANS RESIST THE NEW 1835 CONSTITUTION

In the meantime, the politics of Mexico pursued a chaotic existence. Between 1821 and 1850, Mexico created three constitutions, twenty governments and a multitude of presidents. The most notable of these was Antonio Lopez de Santa Anna, a wealthy landowner who built a strong political base in Veracruz and achieved a heroic reputation in several military battles during Mexico's struggle for independence from Spain. Charismatic, cunning and ruthless, he successfully defeated his opponents to become president eleven times over a 40-year period. Mexican authorities came to rely on his military strength to gather large armies and rebuild them, even after major losses.

In 1834, newly elected president Santa Anna used the power of the clergy and military to establish himself as dictator and dissolved the 1824 constitution, a move that heightened tensions between the Mexican government and the Texian immigrants. The earlier document had focused on a federalist government that granted considerable power to individual states for creating their own state governments and laws. The 1835 constitution was founded on new "*Siete Leyes,*" or Seven Laws, which restored greater power to the military and the clergy and created a centralist government. Many of the states' rights were eliminated and a number of liberal reforms repealed. State legislatures and militias were disbanded.

Fierce resistance broke out all over the country. Yucatan declared itself an independent Republic. Zacatecas took up arms and revolted, but was quickly defeated by Santa Anna's army. Militias in Oaxaca were brutally suppressed.

Greatly alarmed, colonists at San Felipe de Austin, now numbering 8,000, urged their leader to propose a Mexican State of Tejas separate from Coahuila. Stephen Austin traveled to Mexico City and presented the proposal to Santa Anna, who immediately imprisoned Austin on suspicion of insurrection. Held without trial from January 1834 to July 1835, Austin was eventually released and arrived home at San Felipe at the end of August 1835, the eve of the Texas Revolution.

MEXICAN GENERAL AND PRESIDENT SANTA ANNA

Antonio Lopez de Santa Anna, a prominent and popular general in Mexico's fight for independence from Spain in 1821, was elected President of Mexico in 1833, winning by a landslide. Supported by the army and the Catholic Church, Santa Anna led a military coup one year later and pronounced himself dictator. Declaring Mexico's 1824 Constitution null and void, a new 1835 Constitution removed many of the democratic reforms of the earlier document and had the effect of launching the Texas Revolution. A skilled tactician and remarkable leader, Santa Anna dominated Mexico's politics, serving as its president eleven non-successive times during his turbulent 40-year career.

Brutal and ruthless, Santa Anna personally conducted the military operations against the Texas rebellion, killing all Texas men at the Battle of the Alamo and executing over four hundred captured Texas prisoners as they were held at Goliad. His excessive brutality helped fuel the determination of the Texas revolutionary cause, which led to Santa Anna's defeat and capture at the Battle of San Jacinto. Fearing execution by the Texans, he agreed to the Velasco Treaties, which granted Texas the lands north of the Rio Grande and gave birth to an independent Republic of Texas, which lasted until 1845, when it was admitted to the United States.

After a brief exile in the United States, Santa Anna was allowed to return to Mexico in 1837. He soon reestablished his reputation as a military leader, resisting the French in 1838–39. Santa Anna was soon President again, but his harsh dictatorial methods forced authorities to send him into exile to Cuba, still a Spanish colony. At the onset of the Mexican-American War in 1846, Santa Anna used his persuasive powers from Cuba to convince Mexican authorities that he was needed there to lead an army against the American invaders.

Returning to Mexico in August 1846, Santa Anna created an army and quickly declared himself President. But when Mexico lost the war to American forces in 1848, Santa Anna went into exile again, this time to Jamaica and later, Columbia, South America. He returned to Mexico at the request of the Conservatives during the Mexican civil wars of the 1850s and served as President for his eleventh and last time. Overthrown by the Liberals for his excesses in power, he was again exiled to Cuba. He remained there until 1874, when he was allowed to return to Mexico, where he died two years later at the age of 82.

1.3 THE FIRST SHOTS

■ TEXIANS REBEL AT GONZALES

Mexico had encouraged its new immigrants to create their own militias. Weapons and a few cannon had been distributed for protection against the Comanche Indians and for local enforcement of state and federal laws. As a result, the Texians were well armed and presented a potential threat to Santa Anna's repressive 1835 reforms. Determined to quell the rising resistance of the Anglo-American immigrants, Santa Anna demanded confiscation of all weapons held by the Texian militias.

A contingent of approximately one hundred Mexican soldiers arrived in October 1835 at Gonzales, a small community about ninety miles southwest of San Felipe de Austin, both in the province of Bexar. Their purpose was to confiscate a small cannon. The Texians refused to release it, flying a flag with a cannon drawn on it, stating "Come and Take It."

Detail of Mural in Gonzales, Texas, Museum
From Wikimedia Commons, Public Domain. Photo Credit: J. Williams (July 6, 2003).

Two Mexican soldiers were killed in a brief skirmish and the soldiers withdrew. The encounter, although minor in scope, nevertheless encouraged the Texians in their cause and the first shots at the BATTLE OF GONZALES on October 2, 1835, signaled the beginning of the Texas Revolution.

Austin soon announced to the San Felipe de Austin Committee of Public Safety, which would later evolve into the famous Texas Rangers, that *"War is declared—public opinion has proclaimed it against a Military despotism. The Campaign has commenced!"* He concluded his message with *"...one purpose animates the people: to take Bexar and drive the military out of Texas."* Men from nearby communities began arriving in Gonzales, responding to the "Call to Arms." Very quickly, a small volunteer army, the Army of the People, also called the Texian Army, was organized, which would later name Stephen Austin as its commander.

■ TEXIANS CAPTURE GOLIAD

A few days later on October 9, Austin's small Army of the People marched to the Mexican garrison at Goliad, a primary supply depot for the Mexican army. General Perfecto de Cos, Santa Anna's brother-in-law, had been appointed the governing military authority over Tejas, and had just left Goliad with his men for San Antonio de Bexar, the last large garrison of Mexican troops in Tejas.

The small Mexican defense force that remained at Goliad soon fell to the Texians, who promptly confiscated its supplies and several cannons. The new Texian Army, numbering about three hundred, pursued Gen. Cos to San Antonio. Austin deployed a contingent of ninety soldiers ahead of the group to find a defensible location near the Mexican army. The scouting party selected a site near the Mission of Concepcion on the San Antonio River about two miles from San Antonio and set up camp there.

When Cos learned the Texian Army was divided, he sent about four hundred cavalry and infantry to attack the smaller group at the mission. The Texians had positioned themselves between two sides of a horseshoe-shaped curve on the San Antonio River, which left the Mexicans little maneuvering room. Surrounded by trees, the Texians were protected from the Mexican cavalry and with their longer-range rifles, they defeated several Mexican attacks, losing only one man. The Mexican soldiers withdrew to San Antonio just before the remainder of Austin's army arrived, granting the BATTLE OF CONCEPCION on October 28 to the Texians.

■ TEXIANS PLACE SAN ANTONIO UNDER SIEGE

Austin's army soon surrounded the garrison at San Antonio and placed it under siege. They had been joined by about forty Mexican-born Tejanos, led by Juan Seguin, a government official in San Antonio. The Tejanos supported Mexico's 1824 Constitution that had provided greater independence to individual states and opposed the changes initiated by Santa Anna in the 1835 Constitution.

About one hundred twenty Americans from New Orleans, known as the "First Company of Texan Volunteers from New Orleans" were part of the group. The men carried rifles, not muskets, with good ammunition, acted like soldiers and wore grey military fatigues. They became known as the

"New Orleans Greys." Uniforms of grey would appear again thirteen years in the future for the Confederate Army during the American Civil War. The "Greys" arrived with an 18-pound cannon that would play a special role in the battle to come.

Additional reinforcements brought Austin's army to about six hundred men as several nearby communities and American adventurers arrived to join the army

The Mexican army also received reinforcements and now stood at 1,200 men. Cos fortified the town squares and plaza with eleven cannon. But without Goliad and its Gulf Coast access, Cos was now forced to use a long overland route for animal forage, supplies and food, which soon forced rationing as quantities dwindled.

■ TEXANS FORM NEW PROVISIONAL GOVERNMENT

As tensions were mounting at San Antonio and Goliad in early November 1835, San Felipe de Austin became the center for a political convention: the "Texas Consultation." Elected delegates from thirteen municipalities representing Texas gathered to reach consensus on how to resist the "Seven Laws" and the 1835 Constitution being imposed by Santa Anna.

One of the delegates was Sam Houston, representing Nacogdoches. As a young man, Houston had served under Andrew Jackson during the War of 1812, and the Creek Indian Wars (1813-14) in Mississippi Territory. Houston then spent another ten years in Tennessee politics, serving one term as governor, before immigrating to Coahuila y Tejas in 1833. He became recognized as a leader in the resulting San Felipe discussions.

Since many of the delegates, including Stephen Austin, were serving in the Texian Army and currently surrounding San Antonio in a siege, Houston traveled there to meet with Austin and obtain permission for some of the delegates to temporarily leave the siege. Reaching a compromise, all delegates who were not staff officers had permission to temporarily leave the siege and participate in the Consultation. Austin and two other officers remained to oversee military operations while twenty delegates accompanied Houston to San Felipe. A quorum for the Consultation was finally reached on November 4.

On November 7, delegates voted to release a resolution that supported the Mexican Constitution of 1824, which stated in part:

> "...*The people of Texas, availing themselves of their natural rights, solemnly declare that they have taken up arms in defense of their Rights and Liberties which were threatened by the encroachments of military despots and in defense of the Republican Principles of the Federal Constitution of Mexico of 1824... they hold it to be their right...to withdraw from the Union (of Mexico), to establish an independent Government, or to adopt such measures as they may deem best calculated to protect their rights and liberties...*"

While there was not universal agreement among the delegates that this was the right time to declare their independence from Mexico, the resolution did state that Texas had the right to do so. The resolution further declared that Texas had the right to form an army and to grant public lands to volunteers, rights currently reserved for states.

In the neighboring United States, similar discussions regarding states' rights and the independence of states from federal control were also prevailing at that time as a prominent topic of conflict. Resolution of that dispute would not be settled until the conclusion of the American Civil War, thirteen years in the future.

The Consultation delegates voted to establish a Provisional Government, headed by a Governor and General Council, which consisted of one representative from each municipality. The Council officially established the Provisional Army of Texas, to be commanded by Sam Houston.

Stephen Austin was authorized to travel to the United States and seek funding and volunteers for the Texas cause. Leadership for the Texian Army of the People was turned over to Edward Burleson, who had been serving as Austin's second-in-command. Burleson had immigrated to Texas in 1830 after receiving a land grant at San Felipe de Austin and had been an active member of Austin's militia. The new Texas Provisional Government agreed to meet again March 1, 1836, at Washington-on-the-Brazos.

■ MEXICANS SURRENDER SAN ANTONIO TO THE TEXIANS

The Texian Army of the People continued its siege of San Antonio de Bexar throughout November, under Commander Burleson, with limited skirmishes between the combatants. In late November, Texians intercepted a pack train of mules and horses en route to San Antonio, accompanied by Mexican soldiers. Ambushing the group in a ravine, the Texians soon found themselves fighting Mexican cavalry that was rushed in from San Antonio.

But Texian cavalry, supported by infantry, soon won the GRASS FIGHT on November 26, 1835, and the Mexicans withdrew. When the Texians captured the scattered animals, they found only freshly cut grass being carried to feed the animals trapped during the siege. Rumors of gold and silver to pay the Mexican soldiers trapped at San Antonio proved unfounded.

JAMES BOWIE

Jim Bowie epitomized the tough frontiersman who occupied the untamed U. S.-Mexican borderland in the 1820s. As a young man, he made money in Louisiana as a slave trader, selling smuggled slaves that he acquired from the infamous Gulf Coast pirate Jean Lafitte. Card-player, gambler, land speculator and brawler, Bowie was known for his reputation as a deadly knife fighter. His large "Bowie Knife" captured public attention and became an iconic fixture of the Western frontier.

After barely surviving a nasty brawl in Louisiana where he was shot and stabbed several times in the "Sandbar Fight," Bowie moved on to Texas in 1830 to take advantage of Mexico's land grant policies. Using his skills as a land speculator, he began to acquire several thousand acres of land by encouraging Mexican citizens to apply for land grants which he then purchased. He became a Mexican citizen and married into a wealthy Mexican family from San Antonio.

When new policies made land speculation illegal, Bowie became an ardent advocate for Texas independence. He served as a Colonel in Stephen Austin's Texian Army and distinguished himself as a natural leader at the Battle of Concepcion. After joining the Alamo defenders, Bowie shared leadership with Col. William Travis who represented the Provisional Army of Texas, headed by Sam Houston. But before the Battle of the Alamo occurred, the 39-year-old Bowie collapsed from a deadly illness, thought to be tuberculosis, typhoid or yellow fever. Confined to a cot when Mexican forces attacked on March 6, 1836, he was killed along with the others in the final battle.

On December 5, Texians launched a surprise attack on San Antonio and captured houses within the town. Another attack two days later prompted Gen. Cos to withdraw from the city squares and set up his defenses in the walls of the Alamo, a Spanish religious mission since 1700, located nearby. The Alamo provided a good defensive position because of its small size and thick walls.

When Cos began to concentrate his Mexican cavalry in the Alamo, about one hundred seventy-five soldiers from four companies rode away, deserting the conflict. Limited by lack of food and supplies, and now a reduced force, Cos was forced to surrender to the Texians. The besieged Mexican soldiers were paroled and about one thousand of them left San Antonio and the Alamo December 14 to relocate south to the Rio Grande near Laredo.

After Cos' surrender, most of the Texians believed the Revolution was over and as winter approached, many of them left the army to go home or follow other pursuits. Burleson resigned his command of the Texian Army December 15 and returned to his home at San Felipe. Most of the Greys left to join the Texians at Goliad and others traveled to Gonzales. A few remained at the Alamo.

WILLIAM B. TRAVIS

Twenty-year-old William Travis, working as a newspaper publisher and lawyer in Claiborne, Alabama, found himself with insurmountable debt in 1829. Hearing about the flood of immigrants flocking to Mexican Texas to sign up for free land, Travis left for Texas in 1831 and never went back. He set up his law practice to handle settlers' land dealings and became counsel for Stephen Austin's colony.

As hostilities heated up between the Mexican government and the colonists, Travis organized a local militia and became a leader in the Texas rebellion. When the Texas Revolution commenced, Travis was named Colonel in the newly formed Provisional Army of Texas. He would lead the defenders at the Battle of the Alamo and die there. His famous "Victory or Death" plea for support became known as a universal emblem of courage, heroism and self sacrifice.

"To the People of Texas & All Americans in the World. . . we are besieged by a thousand or more of the Mexicans under Santa Anna. . . I call on you in the name of Liberty, of patriotism & everything dear to the American character, to come to our aid, with all dispatch. . . . If this call is neglected, I am determined to sustain myself as long as possible and die like a soldier who never forgets what is due to his own honor and that of his country. VICTORY OR DEATH"

DAVY CROCKETT

Davy Crockett, the popular and famous frontier hero, arrived in Nacogdoches, Texas (Tejas), in January 1836, looking forward to exploring the country, starting a new life there and moving his family from Tennessee to join him. Welcomed by local citizens as "King of the Wild Frontier," Crockett had been written about in numerous books, stage plays and almanacs for his hunting skills and frontier exploits, enhanced by the highly popular play, "The Lion of the West."

Famous for wearing his coonskin cap, Crockett had served three terms in the U.S. House of Representatives, but had been defeated for a fourth term in 1835 because of his vote against the Indian Removal Act, the only delegate of Tennessee to do so. He defended his vote to his constituents, describing the measure "...as wicked and unjust" and he could not in good conscience vote for it, ending with a famous quote, "You might all go to hell and I will go to Texas."

Arriving in Nacogdoches shortly after the defeat of the Mexicans in the Siege of San Antonio, Crockett and his followers soon signed an oath to the Provisional Government of Texas for six months, expecting Texas to soon be independent. The 49-year-old Crockett anticipated being elected as a representative to form a constitution for Texas and he would revive his political career in this new land. He and twelve followers moved on to San Antonio February 8 and joined the other Alamo defenders. All were killed in the final ferocious battle March 6, 1836, and Crockett became an American legend.

◼ SANTA ANNA MOVES MEXICAN ARMY TO ATTACK THE ALAMO

Outraged that his brother-in-law Cos had surrendered to the Texians, Santa Anna organized a large army at San Luis Potosi and began to move it northward by late December. They would retake San Antonio and the Alamo and avenge the family's honor. Santa Anna enlarged his army to about 6,000 soldiers by coercing recruits from low levels of society with no military experience. Ex-convicts, derelicts and native Indian peasants, who could not understand Spanish, were all conscripted into an army that had few professional soldiers.

As Santa Anna pushed his army north to meet the Texians, inadequate food, clothing or medical supplies for the troops took a terrible toll. The expedition, short of horses, mules, cattle and wagons, stretched out over three hundred miles across the Mexican deserts during the worst winter recorded. The soldiers, completely unprepared to function in a non-tropical climate, suffered from hypothermia and many died of cold and dysentery.

In addition to the challenges of the arduous march, many more of the Mexican army were lost to Comanche raiding parties. Exacerbating the situation were the multitudes of *soldaderas*, the women with children who accompanied the army to serve the men as prostitutes, laundresses, cooks, nurses, maids and wives.

"NO QUARTER"

Santa Anna issued an order on December 7, 1835, that any armed foreigner taken in combat would be treated as a pirate and executed, or shown "No Quarter." The Mexican Congress made it a law three weeks later, to be known as the Tornel Decree. Tornel was then the Mexican Secretary of Defense.

As Santa Anna's depleted army approached the Rio Grande in the middle of February, he placed some five hundred soldiers under Gen. Jose de Urrea, ordering them to move north from Matamoros. Urrea was to defeat all Texians along the Gulf Coast, known as the Goliad Campaign, and prevent any reinforcements for Texas coming in from the sea. Santa Anna continued to San Antonio with the rest of his army.

■ DEFENDERS OF THE ALAMO

The number of defenders at the Alamo had become significantly reduced after the defeat of Mexican Gen. Cos and his troops in December. Appeals to the new Provisional Army of Texas for reinforcements and supplies were unfulfilled as the Provisional Government had no funds and the army, with only a few soldiers, was still largely nonexistent.

Learning that Santa Anna's large army was approaching San Antonio, Colonel James Bowie, who had led the Battle of Concepcion as part of Austin's Texian Army, brought about thirty men to unite with the small group at the Alamo in late January. Gen. Sam Houston sent about thirty men, headed by Col. James Travis, in early February from the Provisional Army of Texas. Five days later, on February 8, Davy Crockett arrived from Tennessee with twelve men. Houston recommended the removal of all artillery from the Alamo and the men should abandon the site. But the defenders felt they should hold the Alamo as a frontier picket guard that could alert Texas settlements of an approaching enemy. The Alamo defenders now numbered about one hundred fifty.

Leadership was contested by the men as to whether Travis or Bowie would lead them. Men who had joined the Provisional Army of Texas demanded that Col. Travis be their commander, while the Texian volunteers wanted Col. Bowie. A compromise was eventually reached which gave each of the two men commanding duties of their respective groups, with joint authority over garrison orders and correspondence. Col. Bowie would soon become bedridden by a severe illness, variously thought to be tuberculosis, typhoid, cholera or yellow fever, before the final battle. At that point, Travis took full command of all the men.

Santa Anna's Army of 3,000 attack Alamo defenders, numbering about 200.
Retrieved from the Digital Public Library of America, http://digitalcollections.nypl.org/ items/510d47e0-f922-a3d9-e040-e00a18064a99.

1.4 BATTLE OF THE ALAMO

■ "VICTORY OR DEATH"

The Mexican army, numbering about 1,500, arrived at the Alamo February 23, 1836, and immediately initiated a siege. A Texas courier was able to get a letter from Travis out of the Alamo the next day, pleading for reinforcements, his last words ending with *"Victory or Death."* The letter would become a lasting emblem of courage and self-sacrifice.

Travis' letter, aimed primarily at the local communities of Gonzales, Goliad and San Felipe de Austin, was quickly circulated to newspapers throughout the United States and much of Europe, with dramatic effect. An aroused public increased its support for the Texas cause. Volunteers began to gather at Gonzales, waiting for reinforcements from Goliad.

Col. James Fannin, commander at Goliad, launched a relief march on February 26 of about three hundred men and four pieces of artillery to come to the aid of the Alamo, ninety miles away. But the ill-equipped company (some men were without shoes) was unable to recover from a wagon breakdown. Shortly after leaving the fort, the rescue mission had to be abandoned.

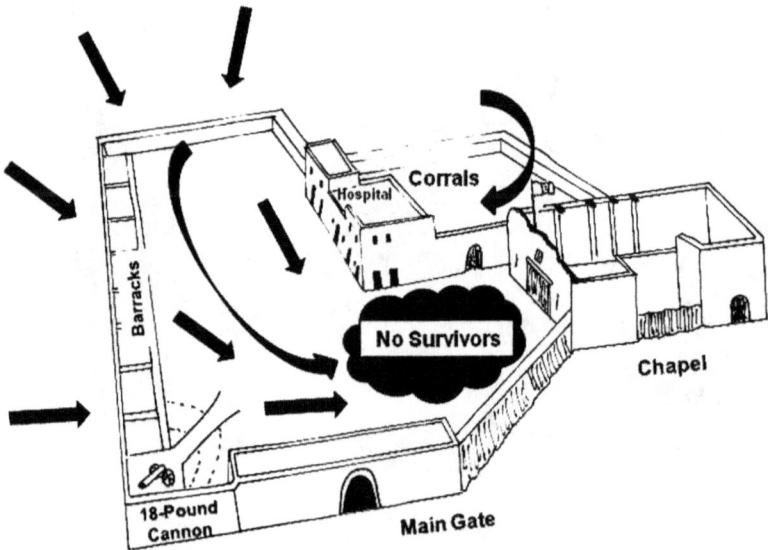

Santa Anna's Final Assault on the Alamo defenders, March 6, 1836.
Illustrator: Sandra Zink

On March 1, thirty-two men of the Gonzales militia volunteers formed the Gonzales Mounted Ranger Company and managed to pass through Santa Anna's siege to enter the Alamo. Killed in the final battle with the other defenders, they would later be called the "Immortal 32."

Various other volunteers entered the Alamo over the next three days, bringing the total number of defenders to about 180. Juan Seguin, Mexican citizen of San Antonio, who had brought forty Tejano followers to the Texian cause, was sent by Travis through Santa Anna's lines with another plea for help.

■ ALL ALAMO DEFENDERS KILLED

On February 24, Santa Anna's army was reinforced with an additional six hundred men, headed by Gen. Cos, who had surrendered to Austin's troops at San Antonio in December. Cos had garrisoned his army at the Rio Grande near Laredo about one hundred fifty miles south of San Antonio. Santa Anna's army now totaled more than 2,000.

Santa Anna continued the Siege of the Alamo with cannon bombardment that weakened the thick walls of the Alamo. When the solid red flag of "No Quarter" was displayed by the Mexicans, with its meaning: "*All who are taken prisoner will be treated as a pirate and executed*," the defenders responded with a shot from the 18-pounder brought by the New Orleans Greys. The cannon, one of seventeen distributed throughout the Alamo courtyard, was mounted on the northwest corner of the Alamo, commanding a large part of the field.

On March 4, another thousand troops from the Mexican army arrived, bringing Santa Anna's total to nearly 3,000 soldiers. He ordered his final assault at dawn on March 6 with about 2,000 men, positioned at three major points on the Alamo. They scaled over the walls like a swarm of locusts.

The valiant resistance of the defenders, coupled with cannon artillery positioned throughout the Alamo and the Greys' 18-pounder, repulsed three charges by the Mexican army in the first hour. Several hundred Mexican soldiers were killed in the attacks. But the sheer force of numbers overcame and breached the Alamo and the defenders were soon overwhelmed.

As the men fell to the onslaught, they were killed to the last man, including twenty-three New Orleans Greys. Women and children and two slaves, Joe Travis and Sam Bowie, were spared. The BATTLE OF THE ALAMO became known as a heroic struggle against impossible odds where men made the ultimate sacrifice for freedom and independence. *"Remember the Alamo"* became a rallying cry for the rebelling Texans in their resistance against the dictatorial methods and brutality of Santa Anna.

1.5 TEXANS IN REBELLION

■ TEXANS DECLARE INDEPENDENCE

On March 1, 1836, with the defenders at the Alamo facing certain death, delegates representing the surrounding communities met at Washington-on-the-Brazos for the Texas Convention of 1836. One day later, the Texas Declaration of Independence was passed, declaring the "Texas Department of the Mexican State of Coahuila y Tejas to be independent." The term "Texians," that had defined the Anglo-American immigrants, now gave way to "Texans," as the new Republic declared its independence.

Over the next ten days, a Constitution for the new Republic of Texas was created, much of the language borrowed from the United States Constitution and the constitutions of several southern states. The new Texas government, structured as a unitary republic, not a federal one as defined by the U.S. constitution, explicitly legalized slavery.

The first interim president, David G. Burnet, was elected and the government moved to its new capital of Harrisburg, located in today's Houston.

■ THE RUNAWAY SCRAPE

On March 11, Gen. Sam Houston, now commander of all regular, volunteer and militia forces in Texas, arrived at Gonzales to find over three hundred fifty men assembled and ready to march to the aid of the Alamo. Shortly thereafter, Susanna Dickinson, with her infant child and the slave Joe Travis, arrived to inform the assembling Texas army that the Alamo had fallen and all Texas men had been executed.

Fearing for the safety of the civilians of Gonzales and the surrounding communities, Houston ordered the city to be evacuated and everything burned, leaving nothing for the Mexican army. The Texas Army (of the Republic) began its retreat eastward toward Harrisburg and the Gulf Coast.

As news spread to other communities of the slaughter at the Alamo and the advance of the Mexican army, civilians began a frantic movement to join the Texans, who became their rear guard and protectors. The trickle of refugees, struggling through cold weather, rain and muddy roads, became a flood of humanity, known as the "Runaway Scrape."

Santa Anna ordered part of his army to follow and capture Houston and the Texas army and the fleeing civilians. The Mexican army, which

SAM HOUSTON

Sam Houston, as a young man, had distinguished himself in the War of 1812 against the Creek Indians, serving under future President Andrew Jackson. After the war, Jackson established Houston as an Indian agent, making use of his extensive experience with the Cherokee, since Houston had lived with them as a young man in Arkansas, learning their customs and language.

From his work as an Indian agent, Houston was able to launch a successful political career, serving two terms as a U.S. Congressman and then governor of Tennessee. But a nasty re-election campaign for governor in 1829, accusing him of infidelity and alcoholism, discouraged him from political life and he withdrew to live with the Cherokee in the Indian Lands (present-day Oklahoma) for two years.

Friends eventually convinced him to move to Texas in 1832 and make a new start. After settling in Nacogdoches near the Louisiana border, he soon became a leader in discussions advocating Texas independence. Given his military background, Houston was named commander of the new Provisional Army of Texas after the outbreak of the Texas Revolution. Two years later, Houston led the Texas Army to defeat Mexican forces under Gen. Santa Anna at San Jacinto. The resulting Velasco Treaties granted to Texas the lands north of the Rio Grande and gave birth to the Republic of Texas. Houston was elected its first President.

now included seven hundred men under the command of Gen. Ramirez y Sesma, reinforced with six hundred men under Gen. Eugenio Tolsa, pursued the Texans. Farms, ranches and villages were burned and destroyed by the pursuing Mexican army.

More volunteers joined Houston's army over the next few weeks, including three companies of Texas Rangers, the Liberty County Volunteers and the Nacogdoches Volunteers. Edward Burleson, who had resigned as Commander of the Texian Army after concluding the Siege of San Antonio, now joined the Texas Army as a Colonel of Texas Regulars. He led the volunteer infantry regiment during the Runaway Scrape and later fought in the Battle of San Jacinto. A few of the surviving New Orleans Greys were also part of Houston's army.

As the number of soldiers in the Army of Texas increased, a growing number of men were anxious to engage in battle against the pursuing Mexicans. But Houston recognized the danger of raw recruits with no military training, rushing into battle. He continued to push the army eastward, determined to avoid engagements with the Mexicans until some military discipline could be instilled. Accordingly, an opportunity to engage against Mexican Gen. Sesma was deliberately avoided, infuriating some of the Texas men who then deserted the army.

■ THE GOLIAD MASSACRE

In the meantime, Gen. Jose de Urrea, who had been separated from Santa Anna's army on its march to the Alamo, had been pursuing Texas rebels along the Gulf Coast to prevent reinforcements from reaching the Texans. At the BATTLE OF SAN PATRICIO on February 27, Urrea's forces successfully defeated a small group of Texans, killing or imprisoning all except six from a force of about forty men. The Texans had been on an expedition to invade Matamoros (across the river from today's Brownsville, Texas), but were captured at a local ranch as they tried to make off with about one hundred horses.

Urrea then turned his attention north to reach Goliad, still occupied by about four hundred Texans under Col. James Fannin. At Refugio, about twenty-five miles south of Goliad, pro-independence Anglo families were currently captive to a group of Mexican-born Tejanos who did not support the Texas rebellion.

This hand drawn illustration of the Goliad Massacre was created by Canadian magazine illustrator Norman Mills Price for an article about Goliad in the early 1900s.
Photo Credit: Texas State Archives And Library Commission, Public Domain.

Fannin sent reinforcements to the Refugio Mission to evacuate the Texan families, but Urrea's troops arrived before the evacuation could take place. A furious battle March 12-15 killed about thirty of the one hundred fifty Texans. Although some tried to escape during the BATTLE OF REFUGIO, nearly all were captured and imprisoned.

With Urrea's army of about six hundred men rapidly approaching, Fannin ordered a withdrawal from Goliad on March 19, hoping to join Houston's Texas Army, now enroute to Harrisburg. Transporting cannon, muskets and supplies, the column traveled less than six miles when they were intercepted by Gen. Urrea and surrounded by cavalry.

Outnumbered, the Texan troops surrendered at the BATTLE OF COLETO. They were imprisoned at Goliad, expecting to be paroled in a few weeks. Santa Anna, however, ordered their execution, invoking his order of "No Quarter," in spite of Urrea's request for clemency. On March 27 a Mexican officer ordered more than four hundred Texans, including twenty-one New Orleans Greys, to be marched out of prison in three columns, to be shot at point-blank range.

A few survivors, thanks to the help of a few sympathetic Mexicans, were able to escape and news of the mass execution reached the Texas army. Houston now realized that his army was the only military force available for combating Santa Anna and saving the new Republic of Texas. The Goliad Massacre and the Battle of the Alamo were now rallying cries for the Texas Revolution.

■ THE TWIN SISTERS

By March 31, Houston's army had reached Groce's Landing, a ferry station on the Brazos River about twenty miles upstream of San Felipe de Austin. The privately owned steamboat, the *Yellowstone* from New Orleans, had been placed into service to provide freight duty between river ports in Texas and the Gulf of Mexico. It was currently under the command of Capt. John E. Ross.

The *Yellowstone* was taking on a load of cotton when the retreating Texas army arrived. Houston pressed the ferry into service to get his men, horses and equipment across the swollen river. Ross accomplished the job with seven crossings on April 12. Houston used the twelve days to create a Texas Army training camp and practiced military drills and army discipline prior to proceeding toward Harrisburg, the designated capital of the new Republic of Texas.

During the interim, two six-pound cannons arrived as a gift from the citizens of Cincinnati where they had been manufactured in support of the Texas Revolution. Transported by river boat down the Mississippi River, and then brought to Galveston by the schooner *Pennsylvania*, they were accompanied by Dr. Charles Rice and his twin daughters, who made the presentation to the people of Texas. The cannons were finally delivered by oxcart to the Texas defenders, becoming the only artillery for the Texas Army. The cannons became known as the Twin Sisters and bore the inscription: *"Presented to the Republic of Texas by the Ladies of Cincinnati."*

1.6 BATTLE OF SAN JACINTO

■ SANTA ANNA PURSUES THE ARMY OF TEXAS

After defeating the Texans at the Alamo, Santa Anna remained in San Antonio while Gen. Sesma pursued Gen. Houston and the Texas Army and Gen. Urrea chased rebels along the Gulf Coast. Continued reports of Urrea's successes, however, began to concern Santa Anna, as he realized his status as military hero and President could be in danger if Urrea became too popular.

Santa Anna left a small force at San Antonio and joined Gen. Sesma on March 29 to pursue Houston and his Army of Texas and end the Texas rebellion personally. On April 12, they reached San Felipe and the Brazos River, crossing the swollen river at Thompson's Ferry, downstream from Gen. Houston and his army.

Santa Anna then led his army to Harrisburg (part of today's city of Houston, Texas), arriving ahead of the Texas Army on April 14, intending to capture the new Republic of Texas which had set up its offices there, and very nearly succeeded. The warned Texans fled for Galveston Island just hours before the Mexican troops arrived. Santa Anna set up camp near the Buffalo Bayou on the San Jacinto River.

In the meantime, the Texas Army had resumed its march eastward along the Brazos and reached a burned-out Harrisburg on April 18 soon after Santa Anna had departed. A captured Mexican courier revealed that Santa Anna was still located nearby with only a small force of about seven hundred men. The next night, the Texans crossed Buffalo Bayou about two miles below

Replica of one of the Twin Sisters
Photograph courtesy of The San Jacinto Museum of History, La Porte, TX. Replicas of the cannons were made by the University of Houston, Texas. The original cannons have been lost to history.

Harrisburg with approximately eight hundred men using makeshift rafts and set up camp in a wooded area along the banks of the Bayou.

About five hundred yards away, Santa Anna's camp was situated on high ground near the San Jacinto River. Separating the two camps was a large sloping ground covered with tall grass with a slight rise in the middle. Two brief skirmishes occurred on April 20, where Private Mirabeau B. Lamar, showed such courage in battle that he was placed in command of the cavalry. He would later become the second President of Texas.

The next morning, Gen. Cos arrived with about four hundred soldiers to join Santa Anna's army, which brought the total number of Mexican soldiers to more than 1,500 Learning of their arrival, Houston ordered Vince's Bridge to be burned, the only access across the river, to foil any further reinforcements. But the Texans did not immediately attack.

Santa Anna felt confident that the Texas Revolution was in its final stages and this final battle would conclude the rebellion. As the morning hours passed, he became convinced the rebels would not launch an assault against his superior forces. The exhausted men of Gen. Cos had marched steadily for twenty-four hours and were not battle ready. Around noon, Santa Anna ordered his men to stand down and the army began to relax. By afternoon, the Mexican camp was resting in a siesta.

BATTLE OF SAN JACINTO, APRIL 21, 1836

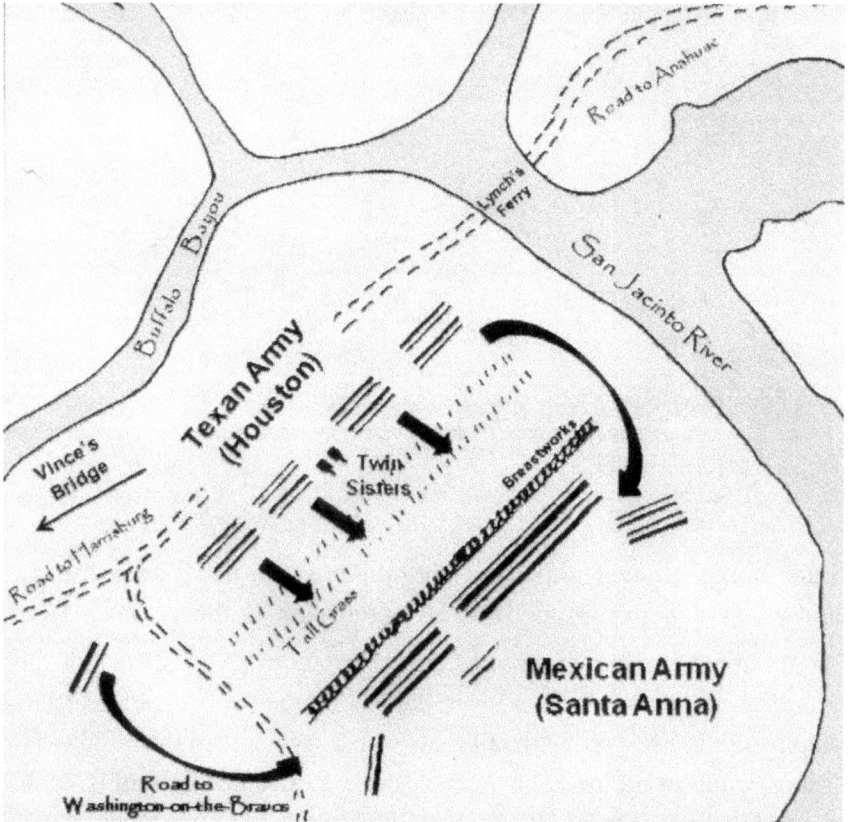

Outline of Battle of San Jacinto, near today's Houston, Texas.
Illustrator: Sandra Zink

■ TEXANS CAPTURE SANTA ANNA

At four o'clock in the afternoon, the Texans quietly advanced in a five-pronged attack across the sloping ground, pulling the Twin Sisters along using rawhide thongs. The rise of tall grass hid their movements. Cavalry, hidden in the trees, assembled to the right of the advance. With the cannons' first volleys thirty minutes later, the Texans broke ranks and swarmed over the Mexican breastworks to engage in furious hand-to-hand combat.

Taken completely by surprise, the Mexicans fled for their lives. Texans showed no mercy; six hundred fifty Mexican soldiers were killed and more than seven hundred captured or wounded to chants of *"Remember Goliad!"*

Santa Anna surrenders to Gen. Houston, wounded in the ankle.
Photo Credit: State Preservation Board, Austin, TX.
Original Artist: Huddle; William H. 1847–1892

"Remember the Alamo!" Eleven Texans died; thirty were wounded, including Houston, whose ankle bones were shattered by a musket ball.

Santa Anna attempted to escape but was captured, dressed as an ordinary soldier, hiding in the marsh. As he was brought into camp, his disguise was revealed by his troops calling out *"El Presidente."* Santa Anna, at the mercy of an enraged Texas Army, agreed to end the campaign and ordered Gen. Vicente Filisola, his second-in-command, to withdraw from Texas to a point south of the Rio Grande with all of the Mexican army.

1.7 TREATIES OF VELASCO

Three weeks later, still claiming to be President of Mexico while a prisoner-of-war, Santa Anna signed the Treaties of Velasco May 14, 1836, in which he agreed to withdraw all his troops and that the disputed territory would belong to the independent Republic of Texas.

In exchange, the Americans would provide for his safe passage back to Mexico. Santa Anna promised to not take up arms against the new Republic of Texas and would lobby the Mexican government to recognize the new republic. Santa Anna was then taken to the United States to be brought before President Andrew Jackson. The now deposed Mexican leader was finally returned to Mexico in disgrace in February 1837.

The United States, France, Belgium, the Netherlands and Yucatan granted diplomatic recognition to the new independent Republic of Texas. Mexico, however, did not recognize Santa Anna's acts done while he was a captive and declared the Velasco Treaties null and void.

1.8 REPUBLIC OF TEXAS TRANSITIONS TO STATEHOOD

After the defeat of the Mexican army at the Battle of San Jacinto and the Treaties of Velasco, the new independent Republic of Texas convened its first Congress in the fall of 1836. Sam Houston was elected its first president with seventy-seven percent of the vote. Stephen F. Austin was named Secretary of State, but died of pneumonia two months later.

At about the same time, two developers bought land near Buffalo Bayou and named the new settlement Houston after the military hero of San Jacinto. The Republic's capital was moved to Houston in 1837 and later to the new city of Austin in 1839 under its second President Mirabeau Lamar.

The new Texas government soon submitted a proposal to the United States to become a state, but the request was declined by the Van Buren administration as the Mexican government had warned it would mean war between the two countries. Mexico did not recognize the Velasco Treaties or the independence of Texas.

Everything changed in 1844 when James K. Polk, a Democrat, narrowly won the election for U.S. President on a mandate that he would expand the territories of the United States. Out-going President John Tyler secretly made arrangements with the Texas administration with a proposal to annex Texas as a state, rather than go through the process of negotiating a treaty. One month later, Congress passed a joint resolution bill to annex Texas, which required only simple majorities in the Senate and the House, instead of the two-thirds vote required for a treaty. Tyler signed the bill into law on March 1, 1845, days before Polk took office.

The Texas Congress accepted the proposed annexation on July 4, 1845, and adopted a new Constitution of Texas in August, which was approved by Texas citizens in October. The document specifically endorsed slavery and allowed emigrants to bring their slaves into the state.

President Polk signed the final legislation December 29, 1845, that admitted Texas as the 28th state. Its admission to statehood foreshadowed the Mexican-American War, officially declared May 13, 1846.

1.9 THE SIX FLAGS OF TEXAS

Spain
1519-1685
1690-1821

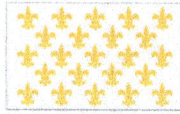

France
1685-1690

Mexico
1821-1836

Republic of Texas
1836-1845
Identical to
State Flag today

Confederacy
1861-1865

United States
1846-1861
1865-Today

With its unusual history, Texas has flown the flags of six different nations over its territory. The flag of Spain dominated the region for three hundred years after defeating the Aztecs in 1521. A small French colony established in 1685 did not survive more than five years. When Mexico achieved independence from Spain in 1821, the flag of Mexico was flown.

The Republic of Texas flag came into being after winning the Texas Revolution in 1836, followed by the United States flag when Texas was annexed as a state in 1845. During the Civil War, Texas flew the Confederate States of America flag between 1861 and 1865, before returning to the U.S. flag at war's end.

The state flag for Texas is known as the "Lone Star Flag," representing the state as a former independent republic and its struggle for independence from Mexico.

CHAPTER TWO

THE MEXICAN-AMERICAN WAR

2.1 INTRODUCTION AND TIMELINE

The Republic of Texas achieved independence from Mexico in May 1836, ending the Texas Revolution that had lasted two years. But its requests to the United States Congress to be admitted as a state were rejected for the next decade as the conflict over slavery in America continued to be focused on maintaining an equal number of slave states versus free states. Texas, a declared slave state, would have tipped the balance.

Further, Mexico threatened war if Texas was admitted to the United States, since Mexico did not recognize the boundaries of the Republic of Texas as valid. They were based on the Velasco Treaties, signed by Mexican President Santa Anna, after his defeat by the Texans at the Battle of San Jacinto in April 1836. Mexico had deposed Santa Anna as President after he was captured and held prisoner of war.

United States' politics, however, took a dramatic turn when James K. Polk was elected President in 1844. As a protégé of former President Andrew Jackson, Polk had adopted Jackson's philosophy of expanding the country's borders, and ran openly on a mandate to extend the country's westward boundary to the Pacific. The vision included acquiring Texas, in dispute with Mexico; Oregon Country, disputed by the British; and the territories of California and New Mexico, possessed by Mexico. It was America's "destiny" to spread across the continent. Coined later as "Manifest Destiny," the concept was shared by a large part of the country.

Four days before Polk took office, Congress passed a joint resolution to annex Texas as a state. The Texas Congress approved the annexation

American Campaigns during Mexican-American War.
Map Credit: Sandra Zink

resolution in June 1845 and a new constitution, specifically endorsing slavery and slave trade, was approved by Texas citizens in October. Polk signed the documents, formally integrating Texas into statehood December 29, 1845.

Shortly after taking office in March 1845, the new President made plans for acquiring Oregon Country and the vast Mexican territories of Alta California and Nuevo Mexico. Polk dispatched U.S. Army Captain John C. Fremont, surveyor and explorer, known as "The Pathfinder," with his guide and scout, Kit Carson, to go west on a mapping expedition. Fremont's official instructions were to more fully explore the central Rockies, the Great Salt Lake Basin and the Sierra Nevada Mountains that Fremont's previous two expeditions had described. Fremont was to define a trail to Oregon Country so that settlers could reach the new land. But Fremont was also given a secret mission, namely, to press on to California if events between Mexico and the United States led to war.

Polk made overtures to Mexico to purchase California and New Mexico Territories for $30 million, but the proposal was refused. Tensions between the two countries over the Texas border continued to escalate. In late fall 1845, Polk ordered U.S. Army forces into the disputed territory between the Rio Grande and Nueces rivers. A Mexican military response to the threat killed eleven American soldiers and wounded many others. Polk, with Congressional support, officially declared war on May 13, 1846.

The U.S. Army continued to battle Mexican forces in northeastern Mexico under the command of General Zachary Taylor between March 1846 and February 1847, which the Americans won. The battle against Santa Anna's large army at Buena Vista in February was the final conflict in northern Mexico.

In the West, American immigrants rebelled against Mexican authorities at Sonoma, California, on June 14, 1846, and captured the garrison. Raising a flag that showed a grizzly bear and the words "California Republic," the affair became known as the Bear Flag Revolt.

Commodore John D. Sloat, Commander of the U.S. Pacific Squadron, located off the coast of Mazatlan, Mexico, had orders to land in Alta California and claim it for the United States if war began with Mexico. With news of the Bear Flag Revolt in Sonoma and fighting between the Republic of Texas and Mexico on the Mexican border, Sloat moved north and captured Monterey, Mexico's Alta California capital, without firing a shot. On July 7, 1846, Sloat announced California was now part of the United States and flew the American flag over the Customs House.

Sailing north from Monterey, the U.S. Navy next captured Yerba Buena (today's San Francisco) encountering no resistance. Fremont and his expeditionary force had reached California in late 1845 and joined rebelling settlers from Sutter's Fort, after the Bear Flag Revolt. Their combined forces joined the Navy at Yerba Buena, now under Commodore Robert F. Stockton.

Commodore Stockton combined the American marines, sailors and militia into an occupational force and promoted Fremont to Major, who was given command of all volunteer militia, now called the California Battalion. The combined navy and militia forces soon controlled all the towns and small pueblos of northern Alta California, with virtually no resistance.

While Fremont and the Navy were claiming land in California, President Polk ordered Colonel Stephen W. Kearny and 2,500 men to take over New Mexico Territory. Leaving Fort Leavenworth, Kansas, in June 1846, the "Army of the West" took possession of Santa Fe, capital of the *Nuevo* (New) *Mexico* Territory, in August. Part of the army remained in Santa Fe to administer a military and civil government, while a separate contingent moved south to capture El Paso and Chihuahua, Mexico.

Kearny, with a small contingent of mounted cavalry dragoons, continued on to California where he joined U.S. Navy and Army troops after crossing the Sonoran Desert. The combined forces defeated the *Californios* in January 1847, the last battle in California.

A second assault on Mexico by the United States Army under the command of General Winfield Scott commenced in March 1847, capturing Veracruz on the Gulf Coast. U.S. forces then moved inland to defeat the Mexican army at Cerro Gordo and again in several costly battles at the gates of Mexico City. The capital surrendered to American forces on September 14, 1847.

With the surrender of Mexico City and its armies to Gen. Scott, Mexico was now under U.S. control and agreed to negotiate an end to the war. The Treaty of Guadalupe Hidalgo, signed on February 2, 1848, ceded Mexico's territories of Alta California and Nuevo Mexico (which included the future states of California, New Mexico, Arizona, Utah and Nevada, and parts of Colorado and Wyoming), and the disputed territory of Texas, to the United States. In exchange, Mexico received $15 million, about half the amount Polk had offered before the first hostilities, and the U.S. absorbed $3.25 million that Mexico owed to U.S. citizens. The United States and its territories now crossed the continent from the Atlantic to the Pacific Ocean.

TIMELINE OF MEXICAN-AMERICAN WAR—An Overview

October 1845: U.S. Army under General Zachary Taylor arrives at Corpus Christi, Texas, outpost on mouth of the Nueces River.

December 1845: Texas annexed as 28th state of the Union. U.S. Army Captain John C. Fremont arrives in California.

March–April 1846: Taylor moves his army into territory disputed by Texas and Mexico; Mexican cavalry attacks.

May 13, 1846: United States declares war; Mexico declares war July 7.

May–September 1846: Americans under Taylor win several battles in northeastern Mexico.

June 1846: Bear Flag Revolt, Sonoma, California. American rebels declare California as an independent Republic.

July 7–9, 1846: U.S. Navy raises American flag over Monterey, Alta California capital, and Yerba Buena (today's San Francisco).

July–August 1846: U.S. Navy and Fremont's militia capture settlements in northern California and move south to occupy city of Los Angeles.

August 1846: U.S. Army Captain Stephen Kearny takes possession of Santa Fe, New Mexico; and El Paso, Chihuahua, Mexico.

September 1846: Mexican Californios retake Los Angeles.

September 1846–January 1847: Taylor captures Monterrey in northeastern Mexico; then moves on to Saltillo and Buena Vista Mountains.

November–December 1846: U.S. Dragoon Cavalry under Kearny crosses the Sonoran Desert to reach southern California.

December 9, 1846: Californios defeat Kearny's dragoons at San Diego.

January 1847: U.S. Navy rescues Kearny and combined Army-Navy forces defeat Californios and retake Los Angeles.

January 13, 1847: Treaty of Cahenga ends hostilities in Alta California; U.S. Navy moves south to capture and occupy the Baja Peninsula.

February 1847: U.S. Army under Taylor meets Mexican General Santa Anna's large army at Buena Vista Mountains. Santa Anna withdraws his army in the night, ceding the victory to Taylor.

March 1847: U.S. Army General Winfield Scott and U.S. Navy under Commodore Matthew C. Perry launch amphibious assault at Veracruz.

April–September 1847: U.S. Army invades Mexico and captures Mexico City, which is occupied by U.S. military until final treaty in 1848.

February 2, 1848: Mexico signs Treaty of Guadalupe Hidalgo, ceding Alta California, New Mexico Territory and lands claimed by Texas to the United States in exchange for $15 million. The United States absorbs $3.25 million that Mexico owed to U.S. citizens.

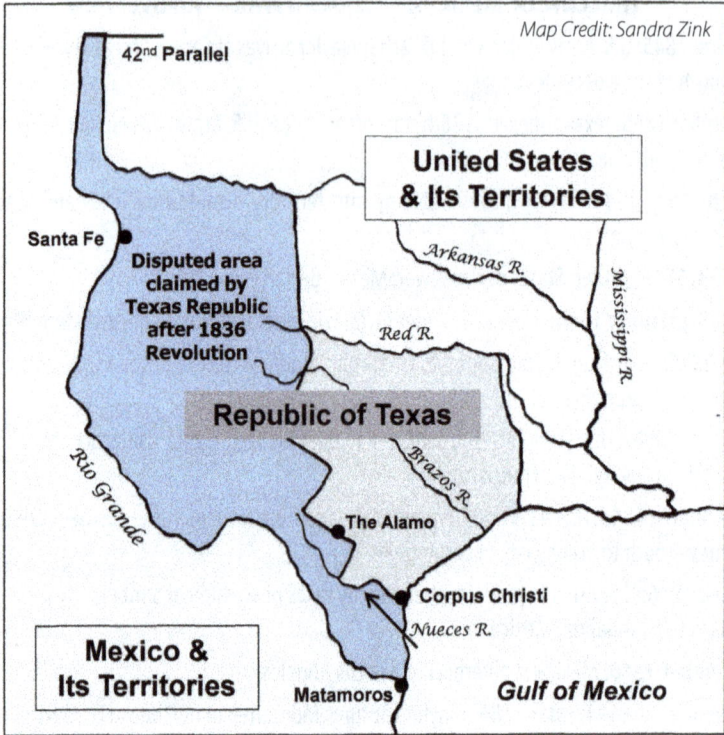

Map Credit: Sandra Zink

42nd Parallel

Santa Fe

Disputed area
claimed by
Texas Republic
after 1836
Revolution

United States
& Its Territories

Arkansas R.

Red R.

Mississippi R.

Republic of Texas

Rio Grande

Brazos R.

The Alamo

Corpus Christi

Nueces R.

Mexico &
Its Territories

Matamoros

Gulf of Mexico

2.2 BATTLES IN NORTHEASTERN MEXICO

■ U.S. ARMY MOVES INTO DISPUTED TERRITORY OF TEXAS

The Velasco Treaties of 1836, which ended the Texas Revolution, were not recognized by the Mexican government. The Treaties, signed by Santa Anna after his defeat and capture at the Battle of San Jacinto, granted the territory north of the Rio Grande (also known as Rio Bravo) to the Republic of Texas.

The Mexican government, however, placed the southern border between the two countries some distance north at the Nueces River, the previous boundary between Tejas and the Mexican state of Tamaulipas. The western boundary, according to Mexico, was the original boundary of the state of Coahuila y Tejas, and not the Rio Grande. The northern and eastern boundaries of Texas were unchanged from their location defined by the Adams-Onis Treaty of 1819 between Spain and the United States.

TIMELINE: TAYLOR'S BATTLES, NORTHEASTERN MEXICO

October 1845: U.S. Army under General Zachary Taylor occupies outpost at Corpus Christi, Texas, on the Nueces River.

March 1846: Taylor moves his army into the disputed territory and builds Fort Texas, opposite Matamoros, Mexico.

April 25, 1846: Mexican cavalry attacks U.S. cavalry in the Thornton Affair; eleven Americans killed.

May 3–9, 1846: Mexico initiates siege of Fort Texas; Americans hold their position.

May 8, 1846: Battle of Palo Alto, Mexico; American victory, Mexicans withdraw.

May 9, 1846: Battle of Resaca de la Palma, Mexico; U.S. victory. Mexican troops withdraw and abandon their siege of Fort Texas.

May 13, 1846: United States declares war on Mexico.

May 18, 1846: U.S. Army crosses Rio Grande and takes possession of Matamoros, Mexico; then moves west to Monterrey.

September 19–23, 1846: Battle of Monterrey with heavy fighting; American victory. Mexican army released on two-month armistice.

November 1846–January 1847: Taylor moves his forces south to Saltillo, Mexico, and prepares to meet Mexican General Santa Anna at Buena Vista Mountains.

February 22–23, 1847: Battle of Buena Vista (aka Battle of Angostura). Taylor's forces meet Santa Anna and hold their position against the large Mexican army. Santa Anna withdraws in the night and marches his army to meet the U.S. invasion at Veracruz.

February–November 1847: Taylor occupies Monterrey.

December 1847: Gen. Taylor given a hero's welcome in New Orleans and Baton Rouge; Taylor retires from Army and runs for President in U.S. election of 1848.

Since the Rio Grande extends some 2,000 miles north to its headwaters, Texas claimed land that followed the river's northern path from El Paso to Santa Fe and Taos, New Mexico, even into Colorado and part of Wyoming.

Mexico broke diplomatic relations with the U.S. when Texas was granted statehood. But newly elected U.S. President James K. Polk was determined to achieve an unbroken expanse of America to the Pacific Ocean. His offers to purchase the California and New Mexico Territories from Mexico for about $30 million were refused. Polk's response was to send a U.S. army

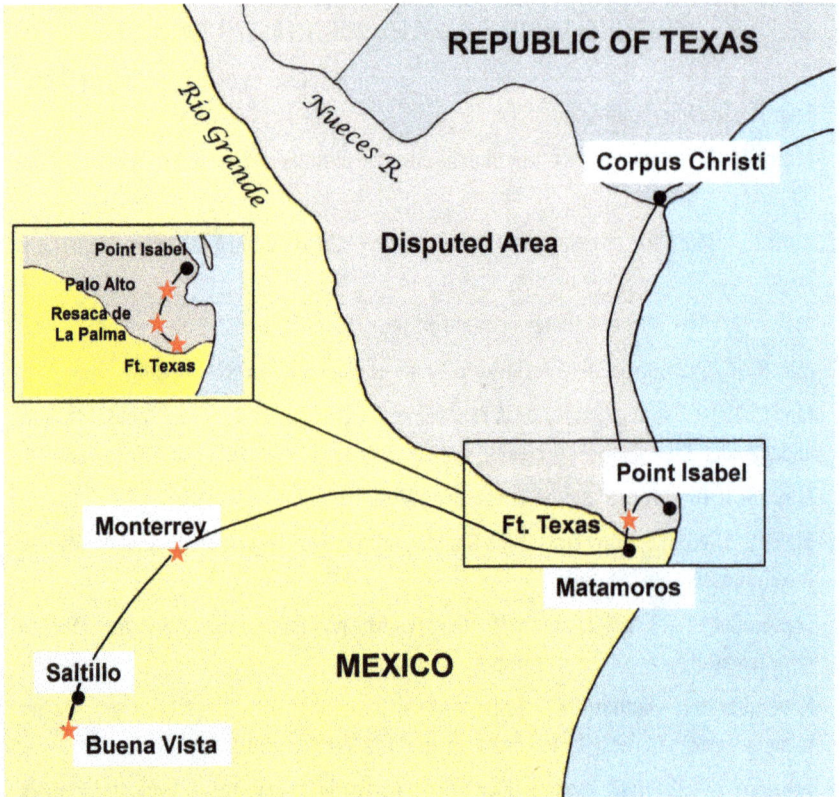

Gen. Zachary Taylor's Campaign, Northeastern Mexico, 1846-47.
Map Credit: Sandra Zink.

force of 3,500 men under Gen. Zachary Taylor into the disputed territory in Texas. By October 1845, Taylor's forces were located at the trading post at Corpus Christi on the Nueces River, but then prepared to advance south to the Rio Grande.

In March 1846, Taylor moved his army south and built a star-shaped earthworks fort, Fort Texas, on the banks of the Rio Grande (today's Browns-ville, Texas), opposite the city of Matamoros, Mexico. Point Isabel, about 20 miles northeast on the Gulf Coast, created a supply base which was used by the U.S. Army for reinforcements and supplies.

In April, Mexican forces responded to Taylor's incursion into the disputed territory with a 2,000-man Mexican cavalry that attacked a 70-man U.S. pa-trol, under Capt. Seth Thornton. Eleven American soldiers were killed and many more wounded or captured. Polk used the Thornton Event to declare war against Mexico with Congressional approval on May 13, 1846. Mexico replied with its declaration of war July 7.

■ BATTLE OF PALO ALTO

The hastily built Fort Texas on the Rio Grande came under attack May 3, 1846, from Mexican artillery at Matamoros. The fort was later renamed Fort Brown in honor of an American killed in the action. Gen. Mariano Arista, commander of the Mexican Army of the North, had been ordered to expel U.S. forces from the disputed territory claimed by Texas.

Gen. Taylor, returning from Point Isabel with ammunition and supplies, heard the distant cannon fire when the attack began. As he raced his 2,200-man force back to support the defenders, he was intercepted by Gen. Arista at Palo Alto on May 8 about five miles from Fort Texas. Arista had divided his forces, leaving about 1,400 at Matamoros, and brought the rest, a 3,400-man army, to

> **GRAPESHOT IN BATTLE**
>
> During battle, cannons could be loaded with "grapeshot," which consisted of small metal balls or slugs, packed in canvas bags. When fired, the metal pieces spread out in a pattern, resembling a giant shotgun, destroying men, horses and any other target in range.

intercept Taylor and his reinforcements before they could reach the men under attack at Fort Texas.

Facing a much larger army, Taylor used light horse artillery in an unusual tactic that had been developed by Major Samuel Ringgold of the 3rd U.S. Artillery. The "Flying Artillery" mounted lighter guns on carriages pulled by specially trained crews and horses. After firing their shots, they rapidly changed positions. Mexican artillery, by contrast, was heavy and virtually immobile in the heavy brush and many of their solid cannon balls even fell short of reaching Taylor's forces.

The battle effected devastating casualties among the Mexican soldiers, with a much lesser loss for the Americans. After losing about two hundred fifty men, Arista was forced to withdraw his troops to other ground. American casualties numbered about fifty. Tragically, one of the four U.S. soldiers killed in battle included Major Ringgold when he was hit by a cannonball.

■ BATTLE OF RESACA DE LA PALMA

Retreating from Palo Alto's unfavorable ground and Taylor's "Flying Artillery," Gen. Arista's troops withdrew about five miles to Resaca de la Palma. The wide deep ravines (*resacas*) and thick swampy brush offered his soldiers an opportunity to defeat the mobility of the U.S. artillery. Positioning his heavy guns and men to take advantage of the landscape, Arista retired to his headquarters, leaving Brig. Gen. Rómulo Díaz de la Vega in charge.

When Taylor's men arrived some hours later on May 9, they tried to move their light artillery forward to the enemy's line, but progress was slow and the heavy brush made it difficult to see their targets. Taylor then switched tactics from using the Flying Artillery to direct charges by mounted cavalry, the 2nd U.S. Dragoons.

An opening in the Mexican flank gave U.S. Dragoons the opportunity to capture Gen. Vega and several officers. Without their leaders, the Mexican defenses were quickly broken. Gen. Arista returned from his headquarters to find his army in retreat and was forced to join them. Following the defeat, Arista ended the siege of the Americans at Fort Texas and withdrew his army south. Taylor crossed the Rio Grande on May 18 to capture Matamoros and waited for reinforcements. His next advance would reach Monterrey about 180 miles to the west.

Taylor's victories brought him to national attention and Congress presented him with a commendation and full promotion to Major General. After the exchange of prisoners between U.S. and Mexican forces, Taylor was praised by Mexican authorities for his humane treatment of the wounded Mexican soldiers, who had received the same care as the injured Americans.

■ SANTA ANNA RETURNS TO POWER

Santa Anna had been disgraced when he lost the last battle of the Texas Revolution to the Texans at San Jacinto, which led to the creation of the Republic of Texas. But after his return to Mexico, the former President was able to reclaim his honor. Calling on his military reputation and expertise, he led a battle against the French at Veracruz, during the so-called "Pastry War," 1838-1839. Multiple complaints to the King of France from French nationals living in Mexico included a claim for damages from a French pastry chef. When Mexico refused French demands for reparations, King

Louis-Philippe ordered a fleet to blockade all of Mexico's ports on the Gulf Coast and capture Veracruz.

During one of the French assaults, cannon fire injured one of Santa Anna's legs, requiring its amputation. The leg was then buried with full military honors in Mexico City. In 1842, the leg was dug up and placed on a prominent monument in an elaborate ceremony. Santa Anna's prosthetic cork leg would later be captured by U.S. troops in the Mexican-American War and was never returned.

When the Pastry War ended with a British-brokered peace, Santa Anna was able to take advantage of his military bravery during the war to reenter Mexico's political arena as a hero and became President once again. His dictatorial rule, however, of banning newspapers, jailing dissidents and raising taxes, forced Mexico's Congress to remove him from government.

Santa Anna was exiled to Cuba in disgrace in January 1845. A furious mob removed his amputated leg from its monument and dragged it through the streets until it was destroyed.

But by 1846, with the defeat of Mexico's armies by the Americans at Palo Alto and Resaca de la Palma, Mexico was willing to bring Santa Anna back from Cuba to once again lead his country against the invaders from the north. He assured Mexican authorities that he would use his military experience to fight off the Americans and that he had no interest in being President.

To arrange for his passage from Cuba through U.S. security, Santa Anna secretly convinced American authorities that he would negotiate a peaceful conclusion to the war and convince Mexico to sell the contested territory to the U.S. for a reasonable price.

He lied on all counts.

Santa Anna returned to Mexico in August 1846 on the eve of Taylor's attack on Monterrey. Once back in Mexico, Santa Anna assembled a 20,000-man army in four months and in a successful coup, was re-inaugurated as president in December. He then led his army to meet U.S. Gen. Taylor in battle at Buena Vista near Saltillo.

■ BATTLE OF MONTERREY

After securing Fort Texas, Taylor led his men across the Rio Grande in September 1846, and moved southwest to Monterrey, using the road that led to Mexico City. Positioned on a 2,000-foot pass through the Sierra Madre Mountains, many considered the well-defended city impregnable.

The Mexican Army of the North, now under the command of Gen. Pedro de Ampudia, had established a defensive force at Monterrey with the remnants of Arista's army. Reinforcements from Mexico City brought his combined forces to approximately 7,000. Gen. Taylor's army of about 6,500 approached the city from the north.

On September 19, the Americans encountered a strong fort, enclosed on all sides, guarding the northern approaches to the city. U.S. troops promptly renamed it THE BLACK FORT. On the southern side, the city backed up to a mountain stream and the Sierra Madre foothills. The western side of the city protected the road to Saltillo and its capture would prevent the escape of the Mexican army.

U.S. Troops Approach Monterrey.
Lithograph by Adolphe Jean-Baptiste Bayot, published in 1851 book "The War Between the United States and Mexico." From Wikimedia Commons, Public Domain.

Taylor planned a two-pronged attack. On September 21, 1846, U.S. troops moved southwest in a flanking movement and captured Saltillo Road and two hilltop fortifications. Simultaneously, a diversionary attack on the eastern defenses resulted in heavy fighting. But by the next day, the Americans had established strong positions on both sides of the city. Gen. Ampudia withdrew his troops and set up defenses within Monterrey.

GRANT'S FAMOUS RIDE

One of the soldiers in Taylor's command was a young lieutenant, Ulysses S. Grant, who was destined to become General-in-Chief of the Union Army in the American Civil War, thirteen years in the future, and later, become President of the United States. During the battle of Monterrey, Grant, an expert horseman, volunteered to ride through the dangerous street crossings to inform commanding officers that the troops were about to run out of ammunition. "My ride back was an exposed one," he writes in his Personal Memoirs. He goes on, "Before starting, I adjusted myself on the side of my horse furthest from the enemy, and with only one foot holding to the cantle of the saddle, and an arm over the neck of the horse exposed, I started at full run. It was only at street crossings that my horse was under fire, but these I crossed at such a flying rate that generally I was past and under cover of the next block of houses before the enemy fired. I got out safely without a scratch."

By September 23, American forces were within the city. Mexican infantry had created parapets, using sandbags to produce low protective walls on top of the flat roofed houses. They would then set off a deadly fire from their muskets whenever U.S. troops were exposed in the street intersections below. Americans sustained severe losses whenever they crossed an open street not protected by houses. Using a technique they learned in the Siege of San Antonio de Bexar, Texas Rangers, referred to as the "Devil Texans" by the Mexican soldiers, punched passageways through the thick house walls and rooftops using small cannons.

Their advances were so successful that by the next day, Mexican Gen. Ampudia and his headquarters were trapped in the central plaza and forced to surrender. Ampudia and Taylor negotiated a two-month armistice that allowed the prisoners to leave with their personal weapons and one field battery in exchange for surrendering Monterrey.

■ U.S. ARMY PREPARES FOR A SECOND INVASION

The Battle of Monterrey was considered a major victory for Gen. Taylor and U.S. forces, but President Polk, a Democrat, was not pleased that an army of 7,000 Mexicans had been released with their arms and that Taylor was gaining popularity in U.S. public opinion. The Whigs (later to become the Republican Party) were encouraging Taylor to run for President in 1848.

Polk instructed General Winfield Scott, career soldier and chief commander of the U.S. Army, to revive his original plan of capturing Mexico City with an amphibious assault from the Gulf Coast. Scott, who had opposed the invasion of Mexico by land through Monterrey and Saltillo, quickly moved forward with his plans to capture Veracruz on the Coast and march to Mexico City by land. To support the mission, he would withdraw most of Taylor's regular troops, leaving only enough to hold the captured ground at Monterrey.

Taylor, however, had other plans. As his troops were withdrawn by Scott, he obtained reinforcements from the U.S. Army at Chihuahua, now under Gen. John E. Wool who had led troops nine hundred miles from San Antonio. The combined forces assembled in mid-November at undefended Saltillo, about 60 miles south of Monterrey. With Wool's men and his own forces, Taylor's strength was now about 5,000, made up of army regulars, volunteers and Texas Rangers.

Battle of Buena Vista: 1847 print based on a sketch by Taylor's aide-de-camp Major Eaton.
From Library of Congress, Public Doman.

■ BATTLE OF BUENA VISTA (AKA BATTLE OF ANGOSTURA)

In the meantime, while Gen. Taylor was battling Mexican soldiers in the Battle of Monterrey and then capturing Saltillo, Mexican Gen. Santa Anna had been rapidly assembling a 20,000-man army and was now on the move from San Louis Potosi in early 1847 to face the American invaders.

With a large Mexican army now approaching from the south, Taylor prepared the U.S. Army defenses in a mountain range about ten miles south of Saltillo near two small villages, Buena Vista and Angostura. The terrain offered good advantages for defense, since the road passed through a narrow valley. Deep ravines on both sides made assaults by the enemy difficult and steep slopes provided high ground for the U.S. artillery.

Leaving San Luis Potosi in late January 1847, the Mexican army arrived at Buena Vista on February 21. But the arduous march, plus disease, desertions and death, had reduced the Mexican forces to about 15,000.

When Santa Anna demanded the Americans to surrender, Gen. Taylor responded: *"Tell Santa Anna to go to hell!"*

Attacking the next morning, Mexican cavalry pushed up the sides of mountainous steep terrain while their infantry deployed frontally along the road. U.S. troops were nearly overcome, but superior artillery was able to hold the American positions. The next day, when Santa Anna's assault broke the U.S. line, the Mississippi Rifles, under Col. Jefferson Davis, were able to pin down the Mexican attacking column, trapping 2,000 soldiers.

A second attack on the main U.S. position was renewed by Mexican artillery. To defend the position at all costs, Gen. Taylor increased the level of grapeshot in the cannons by ordering Artillery Capt. Braxton Bragg, *"Double-shot your guns and give 'em hell, Bragg."* The order would be used as a campaign slogan in 1848 when Gen. Taylor ran for President of the United States.

More than 3,400 Mexican troops were killed, wounded or captured. Taylor's troops lost about 650. With nightfall, the battered Mexicans retreated. When Santa Anna learned that a second U.S. Army invasion was now approaching the Mexican coast at Veracruz, he withdrew his army during the night, leaving campfires burning as a ruse. U.S. troops, expecting heavy fighting the next morning, surveyed an empty battlefield.

This last major battle in northeastern Mexico was Taylor's greatest victory in the war. Occupying Monterrey until November 1847, he was welcomed as a hero in New Orleans and Baton Rouge in December. Running for president in 1848, Taylor won the election. But bad luck prevented him from completing his first term. Taylor died unexpectedly in July 1850, presumably of an intestinal infection or possibly cholera.

Landing of U.S. Troops at Vera Cruz.
From Library of Congress, Public Domain.

2.3 INVASION FROM THE GULF COAST

■ SIEGE OF VERACRUZ

In late December 1846, Gen. Winfield Scott, Commanding General of the U.S. Army, arrived at the mouth of the Rio Grande to assemble an army that would invade Mexico from Veracruz. Many of his troops would come from Gen. Zachary Taylor's command, who had been engaged in several successful battles in northeastern Mexico. Scott reached Veracruz on March 7, 1847, with an army of 12,000 volunteer and regular soldiers, to invade a country of several million people.

Among the boarding soldiers from Taylor's command was young 25-year-old Lieutenant Ulysses S. Grant, who would lead the Union army to success in the American Civil War another thirteen years in the future and later become President of the United States. Accompanying Gen. Scott as one of his chief aides, 40-year-old Captain Robert E. Lee, would become the leading general of the Confederacy, battling against Grant in the final stages of the Civil War.

Wading through shallow water about three miles south of Veracruz, the entire U.S. army was on shore by March 9, with no shots fired. Equipment,

TIMELINE OF SCOTT'S BATTLES TO TAKE MEXICO CITY

March 7–28, 1847: U.S. Army under Gen. Winfield Scott arrives at Veracruz on Gulf Coast and with Navy support, bombards the city.

March 29: Veracruz surrenders.

April 18, 1847: Battle of Cerro Gordo; American victory.

April 22: Castle of Perote surrenders to Americans.

May 15, 1847: U.S. Army enters Puebla without resistance.

May 15–Aug. 6: Americans occupy Puebla. Scott waits for reinforcements.

August 7–18: Scott's army leaves Puebla and advances to Mexico City.

August 19–20: Battle of Contreras; American victory.

August 20: Battle of Churubusco in heavy fighting; American victory.

August 20–September 3, 1847: General armistice to discuss terms of truce.

September 4–7: Armistice ends; fighting resumes.

September 8: Battle of El Molino del Rey. U.S. prevails, with heavy losses.

September 12–13: Battle of Chapultepec Castle. U.S. Marines join army and the castle falls to the Americans.

September 13–14: U.S. Army attacks gates of Mexico City; city surrenders.

September 15, 1847: Gen. Winfield Scott enters Mexico City, places it under U.S. military governor until treaty is signed.

September 13–October 12, 1847: Santa Anna's guerilla forces hold five hundred Americans under siege at Puebla.

October 9, 1847: American relief forces defeat Santa Anna in Battle of Humantla; Americans at Puebla are freed. Santa Anna escapes the country.

February 2, 1848: Treaty of Guadalupe Hidalgo signed; Mexico cedes Alta California and Nuevo Mexico Territories, plus disputed lands of Texas, to the United States.

---

provisions, ammunitions and artillery were brought to land over the next several days with the assistance of light boats.

A battery of siege artillery supported by naval siege guns under Commodore Matthew C. Perry, commenced bombardment of the walled city of Veracruz on March 22 and continued for several days and nights. City officials surrendered March 29 and Scott took command of the city.

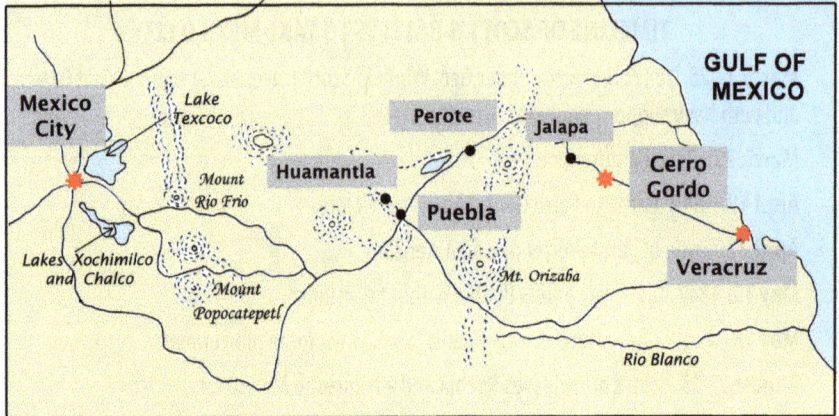

Scott's Campaign from Veracruz to Mexico City.
Map Credit: Sandra Zink

The tropical climate was already taking a toll on Scott's men as hundreds succumbed to yellow fever. Preparations were made to depart Veracruz as soon as possible and avoid more sickness. Leaving a garrison of sick and wounded, the first forces left April 8 for Jalapa, one of two roads to Mexico City. Within fifty miles, leading U.S. forces encountered the Mexican Army on April 11 at Cerro Gordo, one of the highest mountain spurs in the region.

■ BATTLE OF CERRO GORDO

Santa Anna, who had retreated from the battle against Gen. Zachary Taylor at Buena Vista, had marched his army over six hundred miles to meet Gen. Scott and the invading Americans. The Mexican army, numbering about 12,000, had prepared its defenses against their enemy, now approaching from the east.

Scott's army went into camp at Rio del Plan about three miles from the Mexican defenses, and planned its assault. Mexican artillery and infantry had been placed on both sides of the narrow road at Cerro Gordo, which followed a zig-zag path through steep cliffs and around deep chasms. With every turn defended by the Mexicans, Santa Anna planned to slaughter the Americans. If he could prevent Scott's advance, the U.S. Army would remain trapped in the yellow fever zone and the campaign would be stalled in its tracks as more and more men succumbed to the disease.

But the Mexican general was unprepared for the skills of the U.S. Army Corps of Engineers, under the leadership of Capt. Robert E. Lee, assisted by Lieutenants P.G.T. Beauregard and George B. McClellan. All would achieve rank and fame in the American Civil War thirteen years in the future. Lee would become the lead commanding general for the Southern Confederacy. McClellan would create the Army of the Potomac for the Union North and become President Lincoln's General-in-Chief, replacing Gen. Scott during the first months of the war. Beauregard became the first prominent general of the Confederacy and fired the opening shots at Charleston, South Carolina, launching the first battle of the Civil War at Fort Sumter.

At Cerro Gordo, U.S. engineers, under the leadership of Capt. Lee, discovered a rough, poorly defended trail that would allow Americans to get behind Santa Anna's lines, but the steep slopes and chasms were too vertical for animals to tow the artillery. Engineers devised a plan for men and artillery to be moved under cover of night for a surprise attack behind Santa Anna's lines from high ground.

Grant writes in his *Personal Memoirs, "Artillery was let down the steep slopes by hand, the men engaged attaching a strong rope to the rear axle and letting the guns down, a piece at a time, while the men at the ropes kept their ground on top, paying out gradually...In like manner the guns were drawn by hand up the opposite slope."* The backbreaking ordeal required shifts of five hundred men working non-stop for six hours.

With morning light on April 18, U.S. troops created a vigorous diversionary attack at the Mexican front-lines. As the frontal fight commenced, the Americans behind Santa Anna's lines opened fire. The surprise on the Mexicans was complete and destruction was devastating. Mexican forces suffered over 1,000 casualties and 3,000 were taken prisoner.

Caught off guard, Santa Anna had to ride off without his prosthetic cork leg, which was then retrieved by the 4th Regiment of the Illinois Volunteer Infantry. The leg was never returned and is still on display at the Illinois State Military Museum, in Springfield, Illinois.

■ AMERICANS CAPTURE PEROTE AND PUEBLA

With Cerro Gordo in American hands, Scott then moved his army forward to Perote, where the Castle of Perote, a low strong fort, quickly

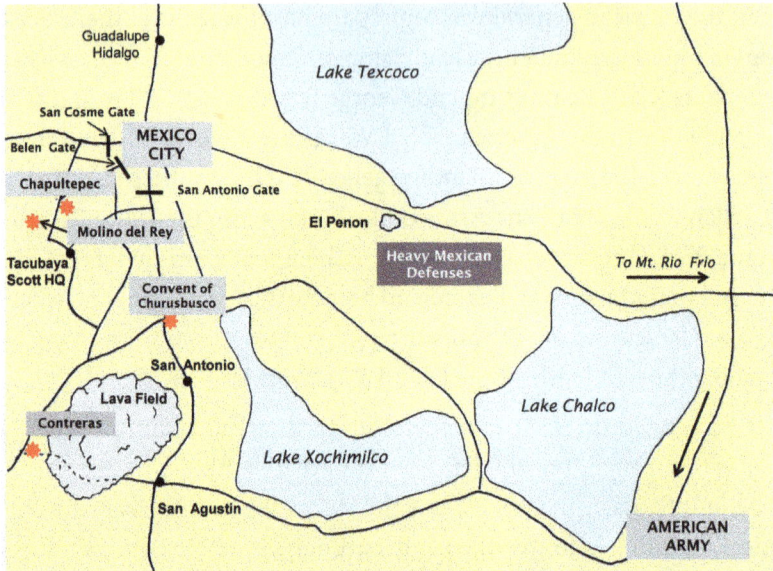

Final Battles for Capture of Mexico City.
Map Credit: Sandra Zink

surrendered to the Americans on April 22, 1847. Scott's army moved on and on May 15, entered Puebla, second largest city of Mexico, which capitulated without resistance. The battered Mexican army had retreated to Mexico City to recover.

At that point, U.S. enlistments were about to expire for about 4,000 troops, which would leave Scott with too few men when they reached Mexico City. Forced to delay his advance while troops left and reinforcements arrived, Scott abandoned his supply line back to Veracruz and ordered all the garrisons at their stations to join him at Puebla. The army was able to survive by purchasing local supplies until U.S. forces were sufficient to proceed on to Mexico City. In the meantime, the waiting soldiers enjoyed a healthy climate away from the deadly tropical yellow fever.

Finally in August, Scott had an army of about 10,000 and on August 7, the march for Mexico City resumed, passing through the 11,000-ft highest point of Rio Frio three days later. The Mexican capital, located six miles farther west, was protected by El Penon, a high rocky mound next to the main road. Santa Anna, his reputation tarnished by his defeat at Cerro Gordo and his failure to win the Battle of Buena Vista against Gen. Taylor, had nevertheless put his military skills to work and quickly built a new army to fortify El Penon with Mexican troops and cannon.

Three lakes protected the city: Chalco and Xochimilco on the south and Texcoco on the north. Causeways, narrow strips of land raised above the low wetlands, supplied the only means of access into the city. Americans took the southern route around Lake Chalco to avoid confrontation with Santa Anna waiting at El Penon. From there, the only direct road to the city was along a causeway separating Lakes Chalco and Xochimilco.

■ BATTLE OF CONTRERAS (AKA BATTLE OF PADIERNA): THE LAVA FIELD

By August 18, 1847, U.S. troops were relocated south of Lake Xochimilco in San Agustin about eleven miles south of the Mexico City plaza. A direct route to the city from there, however, would require going through the village of San Antonio, fully entrenched in a flat plain with no protection for an attacking force.

Contreras (near the town of Padierna) to the west offered U.S. troops the opportunity to bypass San Antonio in an attack against Mexico City. But it was protected by an impassable lava field, called *El Pedregal*, which neither cavalry nor artillery could readily negotiate because of the sharp rocks, jagged edges, deep gulches and impassable surfaces they would encounter.

Once again, Scott turned to his engineers to find a path through the lava field so that the army could coordinate an attack against Contreras. Captain Lee and his team of engineers discovered a mule track that they were able to widen sufficiently for artillery and horses to pass through. With great skill and coordination, the engineers achieved a passable trail and then guided the army through the lava field in pitch dark and a pouring rain.

When orders were given the next morning, August 20, the assault on the surprised Mexican defenders lasted less than an hour and the road to Mexico City was now in U.S. hands. Large quantities of ordnance and prisoners were captured. An American flag was raised to announce the victory and U.S. troops pursued Mexican soldiers, now in retreat, to the convent at Churubusco.

Captain Lee, who had made three night crossings and led the army through the treacherous lava field, was promoted to Colonel, with Scott's commendation that said, "...*it was the greatest feat of physical and moral courage performed by any individual during the campaign.*"

■ BATTLE OF CHURUBUSCO; ARMISTICE DECLARED

When the Mexican troops saw the U.S. flag flying over Contreras, they abandoned San Antonio and set up defenses with seven cannons at the Franciscan Convent in Churubusco. A U.S. brigade pursued the retreating Mexicans from Contreras, and were soon engaged in heavy fighting for several hours at Churubusco on August 20, one of the most severe battles in the Mexican valley. Poor ammunition resulted in two of the Mexican cannons melting and a third falling from its mount. When the Mexican troops ran out of ammunition, they were forced to surrender. It was a major defeat.

Battle of Churusbusco. Lithograph by Adolphe Jean-Baptiste Bayot, published in 1851 book "The War Between the United States and Mexico.
From Wikimedia Commons, Public Domain. https://en.wikipedia.org/wiki/en:Adolphe_Jean-Baptiste_Bayot

The Americans captured more than 1,800 prisoners, including three generals and the San Patricios, an expatriate group of Catholic immigrants of mostly Irish and German descent who had deserted the United States Army to fight with the Catholic Mexicans. They had rebelled against the treatment they received from their American-born, Protestant officers who had persecuted them for their Catholic beliefs.

When the San Patricios were tried in military court a week later, fifty of the seventy-two were found guilty of treason. Gen. Scott later pardoned five and reduced the sentence of fifteen others. The remaining thirty were all executed by hanging during the Battle of Chapultepec Castle three weeks later and are considered heroes in Mexico today.

Losses for the Mexican army, including dead, wounded, captured and deserted, totaled about 6,000 from the two battles. American losses were the highest of any one battle in the war: 1,000 killed or wounded. Gen. Scott did not advance farther to the city gates, but initiated an armistice to negotiate terms of a truce.

The American army remained in place at its headquarters in Tacubaya about five miles from the city as negotiations for a truce proceeded. But on September 2, the Mexican government, outraged at the terms of the proposed treaty, secretly began to prepare for abandoning the armistice. As the next two days progressed, Scott saw the handwriting on the wall, and on September 4, 1847, terminated the armistice.

■ BATTLE OF EL MOLINO DEL REY

Scott's army, located south and west of Mexico City at Tacubaya, observed a large number of Mexican troops at *El Molino del Rey* (the King's Mill), a group of low massive stone buildings, about 1,000 yards west of Chapultepec Castle. The mill was rumored to support a foundry for making cannons. Scott ordered an attack on September 8 to take the mill and destroy its munitions and gunpowder stored there.

As U.S. forces attacked and stormed forward, they were hit heavily with Mexican artillery from a hidden ravine. Although the Americans finally prevailed in the battle, their casualties were more than seven hundred men killed and wounded, including eleven of fourteen officers. The mill actually contained only grain with no evidence of a cannon foundry.

But the battle did provide U.S. forces with a path to assault Chapultepec Castle, a commanding fortress protecting Mexico City's gates, now only about a mile from the mill.

■ BATTLE OF CHAPULTEPEC CASTLE

Chapultepec Castle, built in the 1780s for Spanish military leaders, was now being used as the Mexican Military Academy. Standing at the top of

The Battle of Chapultepec, from the "Pictorial History of Mexico and the Mexican War" (1848), Courtesy of Tennessee State Library and Archives Collection.

a 200-foot hill, the Castle was an excellent defender of Mexico City's gates only two miles away. It contained thirteen cannons and approximately eight hundred men, including two hundred Military Academy cadets, ranging in age from thirteen to nineteen years.

Americans launched a deadly artillery barrage against the Castle on the morning of September 12 which continued all day. The next morning, Scott ordered two storming parties of two hundred fifty men each, including forty Marines, to attack the castle. Using scaling ladders to move to the top of the walls, the Marines were able to storm the Mexican defenders below. Nearly everyone in the Castle was either killed or captured.

■ CAPTURE OF MEXICO CITY

With the Castle in American hands, the U.S. Army immediately surged forward to the gates of Mexico City. Scott's troops pursued retreating Mexicans along the causeways leading to the Belen and San Cosme gates, two of the major entrances to Mexico City. Stone arches supporting the aqueducts in the center of the causeways provided cover for the U.S. forces and also supported American troops who fired artillery from buildings along both sides.

Lieutenant Ulysses S. Grant and his artillery crew hoisted a disassembled howitzer to the top of a church belfry less than three hundred yards from San Cosme Gate. The reassembled artillery, weighing five hundred pounds,

> ### *LOS NINOS HEROES*
> Five teen-age cadets, plus their instructor, refused to surrender at the Battle of Chapultepec Castle and fought to the death. According to legend, one leaped to his death from the ramparts with the Mexican flag in his arms to prevent the flag from falling into enemy hands. The cadets, eulogized in Mexican history and monuments, are dedicated to *Los Ninos Heroes*, the Boy Heroes. They are honored in Mexico on September 13 each year.

fired 12-pound shots at the Mexican soldiers defending the gate, causing great damage.

Fighting was severe on September 14 as the Mexican cavalry defended the city. Casualties were high on both sides. When the Americans broke through the gates, they killed or captured some 3,000 Mexican soldiers, suffering about 800 casualties of their own. By afternoon, Americans held both the Cosme and Belen gates. As night fell, Scott ordered his command to prepare for vicious fighting the next day.

Mexican authorities, however, feared that a battleground in the city would destroy it. Recognizing that the cause was lost, Santa Anna withdrew his army in the night, planning to retake Puebla, currently held by the Americans, and cut off Scott's route back to Veracruz.

> ### MARINE HYMN
> The line of the Marines' Hymn "From the halls of Montezuma..." reflects their participation in the Battle of Chapultepec. The red stripe of the blue dress uniform is known as the blood stripe, commemorating the deaths of the Marines while storming the Castle.

The Americans, expecting furious fighting the next day, were greeted with a delegation surrendering the city. Gen. Scott entered Mexico City on September 15, 1847, dressed in immaculate uniform, as was his custom. The occupied city was under a United States military governor until the signing of the Treaty of Guadalupe Hidalgo in February 1848.

■ SIEGE OF PUEBLA

While fighting was going on in Mexico City, the city of Puebla was guarded by about five hundred U.S. soldiers, who held the convent, Fort Loretto, and the citadel of San Jose, which served as a hospital for 1,800 U.S. sick and wounded. Attacked by Mexican guerrilla forces on September 13, the Americans retreated to the convent. When the Americans refused to surrender, the guerillas placed Puebla under siege.

General Scott Enters Mexico City. Lithograph by Adolphe Jean-Baptiste Bayot, after a painting by Carl Nebel, published in 1851 book "The War Between the United States and Mexico."
Source: https://en.wikipedia.org/wiki/en:Adolphe_Jean-Baptiste_Bayot

Santa Anna's Army arrived at Puebla September 22 from Mexico City to support the guerrillas' continued attacks on the besieged Americans and remained there until late September when Santa Anna left to intercept a U.S. relief column. Gen. Joseph Lane, who had been stationed in Perote after the Battle of Buena Vista, was now on his way to relieve the Puebla defenders. Santa Anna's army waited in the small town of Huamantla, to block the Americans' path to Puebla.

As the U.S. relief column approached Huamantla, four companies of U.S. cavalry, which included the famed Texas Rangers, charged into the town ahead of infantry support. As they broke through Mexican army defenses, their mad dash aroused resistance from the local inhabitants who very nearly cut the Americans down before they safely reached the convent. When the main U.S. column of infantry arrived and rescued the troopers, the Battle of Humantla on October 9, 1847, belonged to the Americans.

Three days later, Gen. Lane's relief forces reached Puebla and broke the siege which had lasted twenty-eight days. Santa Anna escaped, going into exile in Jamaica, and then two years later, to Columbia, South America. U.S forces occupied the captured cities until the Treaty of Guadalupe Hidalgo was signed on February 2, 1848.

TWO AMERICAN GENERALS: A CONTRAST IN STYLES

The individual styles of Generals Winfield Scott and Zachary Taylor, military leaders of the Mexican-American War, could not have been more different.

GENERAL WINFIELD SCOTT

Scott, "Old Fuss and Feathers," in his 60s, was known for his impeccable military appearance and wore his dress uniform with aiguillettes, cocked hat, saber and spurs, when he inspected his lines. All the commanders were notified in advance so that the soldiers under arms would be on hand to salute him as he passed. All his staff was also in uniform and in prescribed order. Scott relied on the eyes of staff officers to describe the battlefield, but his well prepared orders were written with great care and precision with the viewpoint that they represent a history of events. Scott served on active duty in the American military for over fifty years, longer than any other in American history. He was General-in-Chief for Lincoln at the beginning of the Civil War, but old age and infirmities forced his retirement in 1861.

GENERAL ZACHARY TAYLOR

Taylor, also in his 60s and known as "Old Rough and Ready" by the men, rarely wore his uniform and dressed comfortably in the field. He wore a broad palmetto hat as protection from the Mexican sun and a linen duster that covered his uniform. More than one soldier said he looked more like an old farmer than a general, but he was nevertheless known as the commanding officer by every soldier in the army and was well respected. He preferred to see the field with his own eyes and frequently sat on his horse with both feet on one side, one leg draped over the saddle horn, as he studied the situation. His orders on paper were written with a few, well-chosen words, so that their meaning would be perfectly understood. Elected president in 1848, he died unexpectedly during his first term in office.

Ulysses S. Grant, in his *Memoirs*, stated of Scott and Taylor: *"But with their opposite characteristics, both were great and successful soldiers; both were true, patriotic and upright in all their dealings. Both were pleasant to serve under—Taylor was pleasant to serve with."*

2.4 CAPTURE OF CALIFORNIA AND THE SOUTHWEST

Soon after taking office in March 1845, President James K. Polk immediately initiated events to achieve his goal of American expansion into the western territories of North America, currently controlled by Mexico and Great Britain.

In May 1845, while negotiations were proceeding to settle the dispute between the United States and Great Britain over Oregon Country, Polk summoned U.S. Army Captain John C. Fremont, a surveyor and explorer known as "The Pathfinder," to the White House. Fremont had completed two previous expeditions of the West with his guide and scout, Kit Carson, and his maps and reports were held in wide esteem.

Polk ordered Fremont to make a third expedition, to more fully explore the central Rockies, the Great Salt Lake Basin, the Sierra Nevada mountain range and to find the headwaters of the Arkansas River. His expedition would provide important data for the best trails for settlers to reach Oregon Country, a high priority for Polk.

But Fremont was also given a secret mission, namely to press on to California and modify his scientific expedition into a military one if war began with Mexico.

■ BEAR FLAG REVOLT

Fremont's well-armed expedition party of sixty men left St. Louis in June 1845, starting the trek west from Bent's Fort, a major trading center on the Santa Fe Trail. After locating the Arkansas River headwaters, Fremont then proceeded to California, arriving in December 1845 at Sutter's Fort, the first American settlement in California, located in today's city of Sacramento.

Alta California, at that time, was vastly under populated, containing about 10,000 Mexican-born Californians, 1,000 Americans and two hundred or so emigrants from other countries. With tensions mounting between Mexico and the United States over the annexation of Texas, Mexican authorities were threatening to eject all foreigners from Alta California.

Fremont found a group of about thirty American settlers, who were advocating a Texas-style rebellion against Mexico and declare a new Republic of California. Fremont encouraged their cause and on June 14, 1846, the

JOHN C. FREMONT, "THE PATHFINDER"

Captain John C. Fremont and his right-hand man and scout, Kit Carson, conducted their first two mapping expeditions of the West in 1842 and 1843. Educated in mathematics and the natural sciences, Fremont became well known and respected for his scientific reports and maps. His reports of the West's fertile lands, magnificent mountains and rivers were printed in newspapers across the country and stimulated excitement among settlers interested in emigrating to Oregon Country. Fremont's detailed maps of the Oregon Trail, published by the Senate in 1846, guided over 400,000 settlers in the decades to come. His third expedition in 1845 led him to California, where he became a pivotal figure in capturing the region from Mexico for the United States during the Mexican-American War. Settling in California during the Gold Rush of 1849, Fremont became a wealthy man and was soon elected as a Senator from the new state of California. Ambitious and talented, Fremont became a presidential candidate in 1856, but lost to Democrat James Buchanan. He served as a Union general during the American Civil War.

agitators, who called themselves the *Osos* (Spanish for Bears), invaded the largely undefended Mexican garrison at Sonoma, the largest settlement in northern California, about sixty miles west of Fort Sutter.

Raising a flag with a crudely drawn grizzly bear and a lone red star with the words "California Republic" at the bottom, the group declared California's independence. It became known as the Bear Flag Revolt. The bear image remains on the California state flag today.

Fremont then moved his men to the Sonoma garrison and recruited volunteers from the *Osos* to join his now expanding army. The rebelling Californians and Fremont's army next traveled south to Yerba Buena (today's San Francisco), arriving there on July 1.

■ NAVY TAKES MONTEREY AND YERBA BUENA (SAN FRANCISCO)

At about the same time, Commodore John D. Sloat, Commander of the U.S. Pacific Squadron, then located off the coast of Mazatlan, Mexico, had orders to land in Alta California and claim it for the United States if war broke out with Mexico.

Learning of the Bear Flag Revolt in Sonoma, and the fighting on the Texas border, Sloat moved north from Mazatlan and with about two hundred sailors and marines took possession of Monterey, the capital of Alta

KIT CARSON

Kit Carson, born in 1809 in Missouri, became a famous mountain man early in his life, traveling through many parts of the American west, learning to speak Spanish and several Indian languages. His extraordinary talents as a guide, hunter, tracker and scout prompted explorer John C. Fremont to hire him in 1842 to serve as a guide for three mapping expeditions of the West. Carson's daring as an Indian fighter and guidance through treacherous and menacing situations prompted a number of dime novels about his adventures, the first appearing in 1847. Described as a modest, plain and simple man in appearance, Carson was a ferocious and deadly fighter, showing little mercy or compassion for his enemies.

California, on July 7, 1846, an undefended Mexican garrison. Raising the U.S. flag over the Monterey Customs House, the U.S. Navy warships fired a 21-gun salute, the only shots fired in the capture.

Two days later on July 9, Sloat's naval forces occupied Yerba Buena, later to become San Francisco, without opposition, and flew the American flag. The flag was also soon flown over Sutter's Fort and the garrison at Sonoma, ending the "California Republic," which had lasted twenty-eight days.

In poor health, Sloat handed command over to Commodore Robert F. Stockton, who was placed in charge of all land and sea operations. Meeting with Fremont and the rebelling Californians, Stockton promoted Captain Fremont to Major, to be in command of the California Battalion, also called the U.S. Mounted Rifles, now numbering over four hundred men.

As the California governor and Mexican military fled from the invading Americans, U.S. Pacific fleet forces, including Fremont and the California Battalion, sailed south to take over Los Angeles and San Diego. On August 13, 1846, the combined forces of Stockton and Fremont marched into the Pueblo of Los Angeles without a gun being fired and took control of the city. Leaving a small occupying force of thirty-six men, Navy forces and Fremont's Battalion moved farther south to capture San Diego.

Six weeks later, the *Californios*, Mexican-born Californians, fighting as lancers, ejected the small U.S. occupying force at Los Angeles, who then retired to the harbor. The *Californios* held the city for three months before Americans recaptured it.

■ U.S. CAPTURES SANTA FE AND EL PASO IN THE SOUTHWEST

While Fremont and the Navy were claiming land in California, President Polk ordered Colonel Stephen W. Kearny and 2,500 men to capture New Mexico Territory. Leaving Fort Leavenworth in June 1846, the "Army of the West" marched 850 miles to Santa Fe, capital of *Nuevo* (New) *Mexico* Territory, and took control in August with little resistance. Promoted to Brigadier General, Kearny received new orders to move on to California.

Leaving eight hundred men to administer a civil and military government at Santa Fe under Colonel Sterling Price, Kearny dispatched another eight hundred troops under Colonel Alexander Doniphan to rendezvous with General John E. Wool at Chihuahua, Mexico, to the south. American

Captain Archibald Gillespie of the Marines was attacked by lancers, front and rear, at San Pascual; Ink drawing by Arman Manookian (1904-1931), Honolulu Academy of Arts.
Public Domain from Wikimedia Commons.

victories in two separate battles in March 1847 at El Paso and just north of the city of Chihuahua placed the Territory of New Mexico under control of the United States.

Kearny proceeded on to California with a squadron of three hundred cavalry dragoons in early September. As they crossed the grueling Sonoran Desert on their way to California, they serendipitously met Kit Carson, who was on a courier mission for Fremont to inform President Polk that California had been captured and was now part of the United States. With this news, Kearny sent two hundred of his men back to Santa Fe with Fremont's message to be delivered to President Polk and then ordered Kit Carson to guide him and his remaining dragoons to California.

■ AMERICAN FORCES TAKE LOS ANGELES AND SAN DIEGO

When Kearny's weary one hundred men and worn-out mounts were intercepted by about one hundred fifty *Californio Lancers* near San Diego on December 9, they were quickly defeated at the Battle of San Pasqual, losing twenty-one men. Retreating to a hill, they were surrounded and besieged by the *Californios*. Kit Carson slipped through the lines to get a message to Commodore Stockton about their predicament, who was currently docked at San Diego, some thirty miles away. Stockton quickly dispatched two hundred mounted marines and navy sailors to rescue Kearny and his men. The *Californios,* outnumbered, withdrew.

The joined troops of Stockton, Fremont and Kearny moved north to retake Los Angeles. Their combined forces defeated the *Californios* in January 1847 in the Battles of San Gabriel and La Mesa and U.S. forces took possession of Los Angeles. The Treaty of Cahenga, January 13, 1847, between U.S. forces, under Fremont, and *Californios,* under Jose Antonio Carrillo, ended hostilities in Alta California.

With California secure, the Navy proceeded south along the Pacific coastline, capturing major cities and destroying or capturing Mexican ships. Cities surrendered without firing a shot. The U.S. now controlled California, including the lower California peninsula (Baja), and Mexican coast; and the *Nuevo Mexico Territory* of Santa Fe and El Paso.

All that remained now was the capture of Mexico City and the national government. Hostilities in northeastern Mexico continued during the spring of 1847 as the U.S. Army under Gen. Zachary Taylor battled Mexican forces at Monterrey and Buena Vista. Gen. Winfield Scott conquered Veracruz on the Gulf Coast in March 1847 and proceeded toward Mexico City, which surrendered in September 1847. With the main cities of Mexico, including its capital, under the rule of a U.S. military government, the country of Mexico was now fully under American control.

2.5 TREATY OF GUADALUPE HIDALGO

The Treaty of Guadalupe Hidalgo, signed February 2, 1848, between American and Mexican representatives, officially ended the war. The Treaty required Mexico to cede its Territories of Nuevo Mexico and Alta California and the disputed land claimed by the Republic of Texas to the United States. Baja California would remain with Mexico. The U.S. would pay $15 million to Mexico and absorb $3.25 million that Mexico owed to American citizens.

The newly acquired territory increased American lands by 529,000 square miles. Adding in all of Texas brought the total increase to about 915,000 square miles, more than the 828,000 square miles acquired with the Louisiana Purchase. Mexico's loss represented roughly half of its country. About 6,000 U.S. soldiers were killed or wounded in battle and another 11,000 died of disease. Approximately 25,000 Mexican deaths were attributed to the war.

■ HOW MEXICO LOST THE WAR

Mexico lost Texas and the Mexican-American War because of several factors. Inferior weapons were unable to hold up to the superior U.S. rifles and artillery, the best in the world at that time. Mexican ammunition was of poor quality and frequently exploded unexpectedly, making inexperienced soldiers fearful and ineffective.

The average soldier of the Mexican army was inadequately fed, ill-equipped, poorly trained and rarely paid. Long and arduous marches left the Mexican troops exhausted and in terrible condition at the battlefield. In spite of their disadvantages, however, Gen. Zachary Taylor remarked on the courage of the Mexican soldier, by reporting after the Battle of Palo Alto, *"The fire of our artillery was most destructive; openings were constantly made through the enemy's ranks by our fire, and the constancy with which the Mexican infantry sustained this severe cannonade was a theme of universal remark and admiration."*

In contrast, the U.S. fought the war almost entirely with volunteers, who were trained and led by military professionals. The two top American generals were seasoned, experienced military men. Gen. Taylor adeptly identified weaknesses in his enemy's deployments and adjusted his battle plans accordingly. Gen. Winfield Scott, described by historians as the most strategic general of his generation, used skill and cunning to launch surprise attacks on Santa Anna's armies which yielded victories against vastly superior numbers. Both generals had the advantage of junior officers who had been trained at West Point Military Academy as professional soldiers and would later become prominent generals in the American Civil War.

American support of its military, backed by a determined President Polk, provided plenty of money, uniforms and guns to its armies. The American

Navy blocked Mexico's ports, preventing the flow of exports and imports, further reducing sources of support for Mexico's defense.

Political divisions inside the Mexican government, exacerbated by Santa Anna's maneuverings to maintain control of the army and his position as President, plagued the government's responsiveness to military threats. Infighting between generals, politicians and the clergy prevented the co-operation, continuity and determination needed to maintain a consistent defense. Aggravating the situation, various Mexican states, such as Yucatan, were rebelling against their own government. Inadequate financial resources and lack of cohesion and stability within its own government severely limited Mexico's capacity to provide for its defense.

ULYSSES S. GRANT'S MEMOIRS ABOUT THE MEXICAN WAR

"The victories in Mexico were, in every instance, over vastly superior numbers. There were two reasons for this. Both Generals Winfield Scott and Zachary Taylor had such armies as are not often got together. At the battles of Palo Alto and Resaca-de-la-Palma, General Taylor had a small army, but it was composed exclusively of regular troops, under the best of drill and discipline. Every officer, from the highest to the lowest, was educated in his profession, not at West Point necessarily, but in the camp, in garrison, and many of them in Indian wars.

"The rank and file were probably inferior, as material out of which to make an army, to the volunteers that participated in all the later battles of the war; but they were brave men, and then drill and discipline brought out all there was in them. A better army, man for man, probably never faced an enemy than the one commanded by General Taylor in the earliest two engagements of the Mexican war. The volunteers who followed were of better material, but without drill or discipline at the start. (But) they were associated with so many disciplined men and professionally educated officers... when they went into engagements... they became soldiers themselves almost at once.

"The Mexican army of that day was hardly an organization. The private soldier was picked up from the lower class of the inhabitants when wanted; his consent was not asked; he was poorly clothed, worse fed, and seldom paid. He was turned adrift when no longer wanted. The officers of the lower grades were but little superior to the men. With all this, I have seen as brave stands made by some of these men as I have ever seen made by soldiers. Now Mexico has a standing army larger than that of the United States. They have a military school modeled after West Point. Their officers are educated and, no doubt, generally brave. The Mexican war of 1846–48 would be an impossibility in this generation."

Personal Memoirs of Ulysses S. Grant
(published 1885)

CHAPTER THREE

CHANGES TO AMERICA AND MEXICO

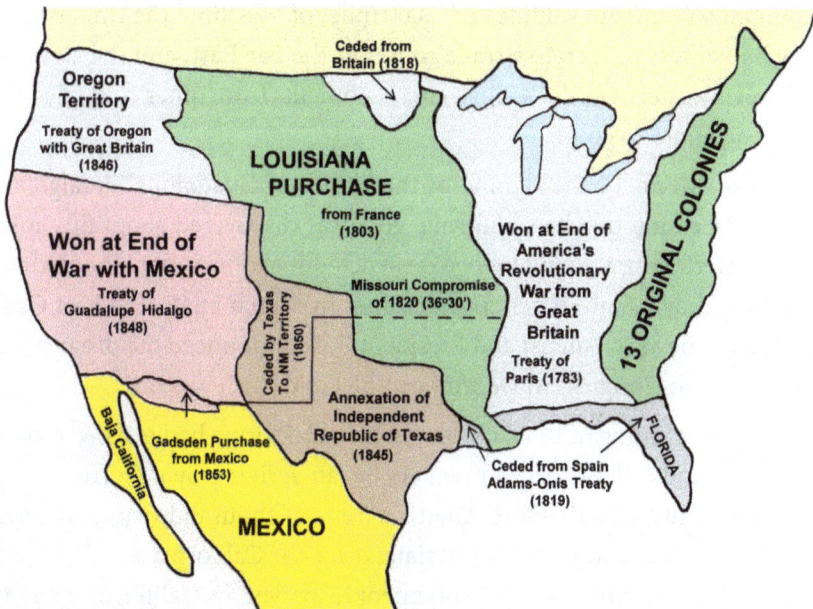

America's Expanded Territory (1853)
Map Credit: Sandra Zink

3.1 AMERICA CROSSES THE CONTINENT

With the end of the war with Mexico, the U.S. was granted undisputed control of Texas with its southern border at the Rio Grande. Mexico's Territories of California and New Mexico were surrendered to the United States, which later became the states of California, Nevada, Utah, New Mexico, most of Arizona and parts of Colorado and Wyoming. Lower California (the Baja) remained with Mexico.

When all of Texas is included, the newly acquired territory to America was about 915,000 square miles, more than the 828,000 square miles acquired with the Louisiana Purchase. In addition, the Oregon Treaty of 1846 had extended the 49th parallel to the Pacific Coast as the northern border between the U.S. and Canada, opening the path for creation of Oregon Territory in August 1848. Combined with the Adams-Onis Treaty of 1819, in which Spain ceded Florida and parts of Louisiana to America, the United States and its territories now claimed an unbroken expanse of land from the Atlantic to the Pacific Ocean.

But the real prize was California with its fertile lands, rivers, beautiful mountains, abundant wildlife and 3,000 miles of coastline. The United States now had access to lucrative trade routes to the Far East, and the ability to defend its western border against encroachments from other countries. But there was more to come.

Within weeks of the signing of the Treaty of Guadalupe Hidalgo and Mexico's Cession of Alta California, gold was discovered about fifty miles from Sutter's Fort at a mill being constructed for John Sutter. The find was announced by a San Francisco newspaper in March 1848. The East Coast carried the news in August and President Polk announced the discovery in his address to Congress in December. The Gold Rush was on.

By the beginning of 1849, news of gold in California had reached around the world and a flood of gold-seekers began arriving by ship from every continent and by land across America. Tens of thousands came overland along wagon trails from the eastern states using the California and Gila Trails. One estimate claims about 100,000 people arrived in California in 1849, about half of them Americans. The rest arrived by sea from other countries.

With the sudden influx of people, California soon had sufficient population to apply for statehood. The "49-ers" quickly approved a constitution and California was admitted as a free state September 9, 1850, the 31st state to the Union. John Fremont was elected as one of its first two senators, and in 1856 was a candidate for President of the country, but lost the election to Democrat James Buchanan.

Between the signing of the Treaty of Guadalupe Hidalgo with Mexico in February 1848 and California statehood in 1850, California was a region without a functioning government. The U.S. military governor, with only six hundred supporting troops, was the only governing force and woefully inadequate. A lawless society prevailed and crime and death were common. There were no property rights. Many of the gold fields were primarily on public land and gold was there "for the taking." Whole populations of indigenous Native Americans were massacred, or pushed off their lands to die of disease and/or starvation.

By 1855, about the end of the Gold Rush, the population had increased by more than 300,000. The influx of gold seekers from Mexico and Latin America, China, Europe, Turkey, Africa, Australia and South America, changed the ethnic diversity of America forever.

About 750,000 pounds of gold had been extracted, worth approximately $2 billion, or about $60 billion in today's currency. The gold brought new roads, bridges and railways, established a large agricultural economy and created a wealthy merchant and commercial class for the state. Major seaports were established on the Pacific Coast at Los Angeles and San Diego. The state motto, "Eureka," reflected California's vision of itself as a place where great dreams could come true.

3.2 CONFLICT OVER SLAVERY LEADS TO AMERICAN CIVIL WAR

The Mexican-American War foreshadowed the American Civil War. Vast new territories were now available for American settlement and brought to the forefront the national conflict about whether the new lands would be slave states or free. Missouri had been admitted as a slave state in 1820, concurrently with Maine as a free state, so that the status of an equal number of slave states versus free would be maintained. Any imbalance in that equation would alter the power in the United States Senate, since each state elected two senators, according to the U.S. Constitution.

The admission of Maine and Missouri had been achieved with the passage of the Missouri Compromise of 1820, which prohibited the admission of slave states from Louisiana Territory north of latitude 36°30′, Missouri's southern border, except in Missouri itself.

But slavery in the new territories would violate the Missouri Compromise of 1820. A further complication was that the Texas Annexation resolution required that any new states resulting from Texas land would be free. Acrimonious debate intensified as proslavery proponents fought the antislavery activists.

The Compromise of 1850 was finally passed as a series of separate laws in early 1850 after two years of heated debate. California was admitted as a free state on the heels of a massive influx of a new population of Gold Rush adventurers in 1849. But two new territories, Utah and New Mexico, would be able to determine by popular vote their status as slave or free, with no interference from the federal government.

Congress compensated Texas with $10 million to give up its claim to western territories in New Mexico and move its northern border south to latitude 36°30', so that it would not violate the Missouri Compromise of 1820.

The most contentious issue of the Compromise of 1850 was the Fugitive Slave Law, which enacted severe punishments on citizens and law enforcement officials if they assisted escaped slaves. In the end, the Northern public refused to enforce it.

Tensions accelerated with passage of the Kansas-Nebraska Act in 1854, which created two new territories, Kansas and Nebraska. The Act allowed each state to determine its status as slave or free, nullifying the Missouri Compromise of 1820. Violent uprisings in "Bleeding Kansas" occurred as proslavery and antislavery advocates collided.

With the election of Abraham Lincoln as President in November 1860 and his public stance against the introduction of slavery into the new territories, Southern leadership advocated secession from the Union. South Carolina seceded in December 1860, followed by ten more states the following spring, including Texas.

The Confederate States of America declared war on the Union April 12, 1861. The American Civil War would last four years, costing the lives of over 620,000 soldiers and uncounted civilians. A decimated South would require years to recover its loss of infrastructure and develop an economy that was not based on slave labor. The 13th Amendment to the Constitution, ending slavery forever in the United States, was officially ratified by the end of 1865.

3.3 U.S. SOLDIERS BECOME FUTURE CIVIL WAR GENERALS

Numerous soldiers in the Mexican-American War would become senior generals in the American Civil War, thirteen years in the future. As combatants confronted each other, many soldiers found themselves facing their former comrades in battle.

■ UNION GENERALS

ULYSSES S. GRANT, a young lieutenant in the Mexican-American War, served as a junior officer under both Generals Zachary Taylor and Winfield Scott. In the American Civil War, Grant would become chief General of the United States Army, leading the final battles against Confederate General Robert E. Lee, which finally ended the American Civil War in 1865. Grant later became U.S. President, serving two terms.

JOHN C. FREMONT, "The Pathfinder," began in the U.S. Army as a surveyor and explorer of new territories in the West. With the advent of the Mexican-American War, he took an active role in the conflicts in California and assumed more authority than had been granted, which led to a military court-martial. His dishonorable discharge, however, was quickly commuted by President James K. Polk. A Republican candidate in the 1856 Presidential election, he lost to Democrat James Buchanan. When the American Civil War broke out, Fremont reenlisted in the army and Lincoln promoted him to Major General to lead the Department of the West.

JOSEPH HOOKER served in staff positions under both Generals Taylor and Scott during the Mexican-American War. Wounded at Veracruz, Monterrey and Chapultepec, he won promotion to colonel before the end of the war. Although known for wild drunken parties and being a ladies' man in his private life, he was an aggressive commander in a number of battles in the Civil War. His military career was damaged, however, by his tendency to challenge his commanding officers. By resigning his command of the Army of the Potomac over a disagreement with Lincoln, he lost the opportunity to lead the Battle of Gettysburg.

GEORGE B. MCCLELLAN, a young artillery lieutenant in 1846, serving under both Taylor and Scott in the Mexican-American War, became a pivotal figure in the American Civil War. A supreme organizer, McClellan, under President Lincoln, created the Army of the Potomac into a well-trained and organized fighting unit. He advanced to the position of General-in-Chief of the Union Army in the first months of the war, displacing the aging Gen. Winfield Scott. His successes in the war, however, were limited by his unwillingness to engage his troops in battle and he was eventually removed from command.

GEORGE G. MEADE, a junior officer in the northeastern Mexican battles under Taylor, was promoted for gallant conduct in the Battle of Monterrey. He is best known for his role in the American Civil War as the commanding general at the Battle of Gettysburg, defeating Confederate forces there under Robert E. Lee. He later served as Grant's chief general in the final battles of the Civil War.

GEORGE THOMAS distinguished himself in the Mexican-American War in battles at Fort Texas, Resaca de la Palma, Monterrey, and Buena Vista, earning praise from Gen. Taylor for his light artillery unit. A slow, deliberate general in the Civil War, he became known as the "Rock of Chickamauga," after saving the Union army from being routed by the Confederates in that battle. His southern Virginia family never forgave him for fighting against the Confederacy.

JOHN E. WOOL served as an officer for the U.S. Army during the War of 1812, the Mexican-American War and the American Civil War. In the Mexican-American War, he led the expedition from Chihuahua to join General Zachary Taylor in the Battle of Buena Vista. After the battle, he commanded the occupation forces of northern Mexico. At the beginning of the Civil War, at age seventy-seven, he led the Department of Virginia and prevented the capture of Fort Monroe by Confederate forces. Retired two years later, Wool was the oldest active commanding general in either army.

■ CONFEDERATE GENERALS

ROBERT E. LEE distinguished himself as the Chief Engineer under General Winfield Scott in the Mexican-American War, earning promotions after the Battles of Cerro Gordo and Contreras. When hostilities began in the American Civil War, Gen. Scott offered Lee the top command post for the Union Army, but Lee refused. Although he opposed secession from the Union, he would not draw his sword against his native Virginia. Lee would lead the

Northern Army of Virginia from 1862 to the end of the war, surrendering to Gen. Grant at Appomattox after a long and bloody struggle.

P.G.T. (PIERRE-GUSTAVE TOUTANT) BEAUREGARD earned promotions to captain and major under Gen. Scott during the fighting outside Mexico City in the Mexican-American War and later became a senior general for the Confederacy. Beauregard was the commanding officer who fired the opening shots at Fort Sumter, the onset of the American Civil War.

BRAXTON BRAGG, a career U.S. Army officer, noted for his artillery performance in the Battle of Buena Vista in Mexico, would later become a general in the Confederate States Army. Promoted for bravery and distinguished conduct in the Mexican-American War, he did not achieve the same reputation in the Civil War.

JEFFERSON DAVIS, commander of the Mississippi Rifles Regiment in the Mexican-American War, led his regiment to capture 2,000 Mexican soldiers in the Battle of Buena Vista, turning the battle for the day. Davis would later become president of the Confederate States of America.

STONEWALL JACKSON, who distinguished himself in the Battle of Mexico City, would become one of the Confederacy's most famous generals, second only to Gen. Lee. Jackson's performances during the Civil War became legendary. He was a master of the surprise attack, driving his men in hard marches that achieved extraordinary feats of military genius. Known for unwavering courage and tenacity, he was nicknamed "Stonewall" when he and his men held the line against deadly Union assaults. His death from friendly fire prompted Lee to say, *"I've lost my right arm."*

ALBERT SIDNEY JOHNSTON, a graduate of West Point, had a full military career, which included fighting with the Texas Army during its war of independence, the Mexican-American War in the Battles of Monterrey and Buena Vista, various wars against the Indians and in the American Civil War. Joining the Confederacy in 1861, he was leading the battle at Shiloh in 1862 when he was wounded in the leg and bled to death on the field, not realizing the wound was mortal. The highest-ranking officer to be killed in the war, he was considered the most capable general in the country at the time. Davis said of his loss *"...it was the turning point of our fate."*

JOSEPH E. JOHNSTON served under Gen. Scott and fought in the Battles of Cerro Gordo, Contreras, Churubusco and Chapultepec. He resigned from the U.S. Army at the onset of the Civil War, the highest ranking U.S. officer to do so, to become a senior general for the Confederacy. Wounded during the Virginia Peninsula Campaign, he was later assigned to lead the Army of Tennessee against William Tecumseh Sherman during the Atlanta Campaign. After a number of defeats by Sherman, Johnston was transferred to the Carolinas, where he eventually surrendered the last of the Confederate armies to Sherman, thus bringing the final conclusion to the war.

JAMES LONGSTREET served under Gen. Scott during the Mexican-American War, earning a promotion for his performance at the Battles of Contreras, Churubusco and Chapultepec. He would become one of Robert E. Lee's most trusted generals in the Confederate army. Good friends with Ulysses S. Grant during their days of study at West Point, both survived the war and continued to be friends after the war's conclusion.

GEORGE E. PICKETT carried the United States colors in the Battle of Chapultepec during the Mexican-American War. During the Civil War, he was one of Gen. Lee's trusted generals, but became best known for the infamous Pickett's charge at Gettysburg, where he lost half his men.

AMBROSE POWELL (A.P.) HILL, a native Virginian, served in the closing stages of the Mexican-American War and then the Seminole Indian Wars in Florida, before joining the Confederate States Army. Mentored by Stonewall Jackson, he became one of Lee's valued generals, gaining distinction in battles at Second Bull Run, Antietam and Fredericksburg. He was killed at the end of the Civil War during the Union Army's final offensives at Petersburg.

STERLING "OLD PAP" PRICE was a colonel in the Missouri Volunteer Cavalry when his regiment joined Stephen Kearny's forces in the capture of Santa Fe during the Mexican-American War. Price was appointed military governor of New Mexico Territory when Kearny left for California. After the war, Price served as governor of Missouri and the state's Bank Commissioner until 1861. With the onset of the Civil War, he initially opposed secession, but switched loyalties when pro-Union forces seized the state's militia. His attempts in several battles to change Missouri from a state that supported the Union to one supporting the Confederacy failed.

3.4 MEXICO'S REFORMS LEAD TO ITS OWN CIVIL WARS

Mexico lost half its country at the end of the Mexican American War, leaving a demoralized and damaged population. An estimated 25,000 Mexican deaths were attributed to the war. The massive conscription of peasants into the Mexican armies significantly diminished agricultural and mineral production for years.

Extensive damage and destruction in a number of cities, port facilities and roads reduced internal and external trade and government revenues plummeted. Mexico's average economic growth lagged behind that of other countries, particularly when compared to the United States.

The humiliating defeat of Mexico by the Americans, in what Mexicans refer to as the "War of the U.S. Invasion," prompted Mexico's political leaders to campaign for new reforms in their government. Two opposing parties emerged: the Conservatives, comprised of the powerful Catholic Church and the military, and the Liberals, who advocated a secular democracy that eliminated the special privileges enjoyed by the Church and the Army. Liberal reforms supported public education separate from the church and the breakup of lands owned by the Catholic Church to be redistributed in the rural and indigenous communities. Conservatives advocated a centralist government that preserved their traditional roles of power and land ownership.

As the two positions became more extreme, the Conservatives seized power with a coup in Mexico City in 1853. Military leader Santa Anna, who had escaped the country after the fall of Mexico City in the Mexican-American War, was invited to return from exile in South America to lead the country as President for his eleventh and final time. But this period would be his downfall.

Santa Anna soon declared himself dictator-for-life and sold territory to the United States for $10 million, known as the Gadsden Purchase, which added 29,000 square miles to the states of Arizona and New Mexico. Pocketing government funds, his corruption, and excessive abuses of power resulted in a liberal rebellion in 1855 and Santa Anna fled again into exile in Cuba. Found guilty of treason *in absentia*, all his estates were confiscated by the government. He returned to Mexico in 1874 under a general amnesty, impoverished and virtually blind, where he died two years later at the age of 82. He was buried with full military honors.

The Liberals, once in power, launched a new program in 1855, the Reform, to abolish the special privileges of the church and military. A new Constitution and secular government were installed in 1857, removing the Catholic Church as the official and exclusive religion for the country. The Conservatives fought back, launching the War of the Reform and seized power again in 1858.

Liberals set up a separate government at Veracruz and continued to fight, making steady gains in the civil war. In 1861, the defeated Conservatives were forced to flee Mexico City and Benito Juarez, a full-blooded Zapotec Indian, leader of the Liberals, became president.

The devastated Mexican economy forced Juarez to issue a moratorium on all foreign debt for two years. Britain and Spain agreed to negotiate payment, but France invaded the country in April 1862 with a 6,500-man army. The smaller Mexican army, numbering about 4,500, was able to chase the French from the field in the Battle of Puebla on May 5, 1862. The battle, immortalized as a national holiday known as "Cinco de Mayo," continues to be celebrated in Mexican and American communities today.

The victory was short-lived, however, as the French returned a year later, with an army of 30,000 troops, and successfully defeated Juarez, who was forced to set up a government-in-exile in Chihuahua. The French installed Maximillian I as Emperor of Mexico in 1864, which lasted until 1867 when he was deposed and executed.

Juarez entered the city on June 5, 1867, to reestablish a liberalized Mexican government, which was sustained until his death in 1872.

But dictatorial rule returned in 1876 under the Presidency of General Porfirio Diaz, famous for leading the cavalry charge at *Cinco de Mayo*. Exercising rigid control for thirty-five years, Diaz implemented modern economic policies that largely enriched the wealthy upper class.

Peasants, suffering under Diaz' repressive rule, were reduced to bare survival and many died. His abuse of power to win the presidency in the rigged 1910 election launched the Mexican Revolution, or the "Mexican

Civil War," which lasted until 1920, when a constitutional republic was established, ending the rule of Mexico's dictatorships.

3.5 THE LEGACY

Texas, once a part of Mexico, but populated with tough, independent settlers, succeeded in establishing its own Republic after defeating Mexico's most famous general and President, Antonio Lopez de Santa Anna. The reputation of Texas as a fierce independent Republic only grew over the next decade as the Texas Rangers enforced frontier justice in the Lone Star Republic.

Rangers innovated the technique of aiming, firing and reloading a Colt revolver from horseback, a practice soon adopted by the military. Embraced by U.S. marshals, sheriffs, gunslingers, cowboys and adventurers, the technique became an icon of America's Old West frontier.

When Texas was admitted as the 28th state to the Union, conflict over the border between the United States and Mexico, triggered the Mexican-American War in 1846. The American victory, two years later, captured vast new territories from Mexico, including the prize of California. A new border separating the two countries provided American settlers and adventurers with an unbroken expanse across the continent, doubling the population from twenty-three million to nearly forty million people by 1870.

California gold attracted hundreds of thousands of new immigrants, who demanded new infrastructure for improved communications and connections to the rest of the United States. Roads, railroads and cities rapidly appeared. The transcontinental railroad reached California in 1869 and fueled an economic boon.

The American economy entered the world stage.

For Mexico, on the other hand, its loss from the war was profound. Mexico lost half its territory and its national pride. Turmoil and political instability prevailed through the 19th and much of the 20th centuries. Its central government, weak and unstable, would undergo continual chaotic transformations over many decades, as the church, military and liberal factions vied for power and control. Dictatorships and corruption dominated Mexican politics.

Mexican citizens, living in the territories taken over by the United States, were offered American citizenship, but in reality, many were discriminated against by their American neighbors and treated as second-class citizens. Unfairly represented in the courts of law, many lost their property.

In the United States, the addition of large western territories brought the conflict over slavery to the forefront. Prior to the Mexican-American War, antislavery advocates had been able to contain slavery within the Southern states through two legislative acts. The Northwest Ordinance of 1787 prohibited slavery in Northwest Territory, bounded by the upper Mississippi River to the west and the Ohio River to the south. The Missouri Compromise of 1820 prohibited slavery in any new states from Louisiana Territory that were north of Missouri's southern border, except in Missouri itself.

The newly acquired territories ceded from Mexico changed all that. Abolitionists argued that if slavery was allowed in the new territories, it would expand throughout the country and violate the Missouri Compromise. Proslavery proponents argued that slavery was essential to the economy and necessary for America's expansion. Antislavery proponents clashed with proslavery advocates all through the 1850s. After passage of the Kansas-Nebraska Act in 1854, violent conflicts in "Bleeding Kansas" raised the level of confrontation.

The long-held beliefs and passions of the two opposing groups finally erupted in 1861 with the onset of the American Civil War, which lasted four years and cost the lives of more than 620,000 soldiers. Some more recent estimates place the figure much higher, perhaps as many as 800,000 deaths. More than one in four soldiers never returned home, and it is estimated that one in thirteen was missing an arm or leg or both. Since recruitment of soldiers frequently grouped men from a specific region, some communities lost nearly all their young men.

For the American South, with its smaller population, the loss of young men was particularly severe, not only for the reduced ability to recover damaged property and livelihoods that were destroyed by the war, but also for the lack of marriageable partners. The impact on family formation as a fundamental feature of Southern life and society was felt for decades.

Most of the fighting occurred in the South, and destroyed much of its infrastructure, including railroads, towns and personal property, and decimated the livestock population. The economy of the South, largely based on cotton and slavery, was devastated. The North, however, had suffered very little from the damages caused by clashing armies and many industries that supported the war reaped major benefits.

Freed black slaves struggled to find the means to support themselves and many suffered from the cruelty of white domination. Sharecropping, in the hands of unscrupulous landlords, became another name for slavery. Politically, federal troops protected the civil rights of black Americans during Reconstruction between 1865 and 1877 and many were elected to public office. But in 1877 federal troops were withdrawn and Southern whites now dominated the political power. State laws were passed to restrict voting rights of black citizens and prevent them from serving in public office or on juries. These "Jim Crow" laws enforced racial segregation in schools and all public places and prevailed until 1964 with the passage of the Civil Rights Act and the Voting Rights Act of 1965.

The Union had been preserved and ended slavery, but a passionate bitterness, for some, would remain for generations.

While the Texas Revolution was a heroic struggle against a despotic and brutal dictator, the Mexican-American War that followed in its wake was initiated by America's determination to acquire more land. Without a strong Mexican government to defend its citizens, the far-flung territories of Alta California and Nuevo Mexico were vulnerable.

British ships off the California coast fed U.S. fears that Britain would try to annex California and extend its reach into the North American continent. Rumors that the British were supporting Mexican troops in California only added to the anxiety. In the 1840s, only a small Mexican population occupied California, weakly attached to a fragile economy and an ineffective government over two thousand miles away.

California, unprotected, was there for the taking.

President Polk, elected in 1844 on a mandate to expand America's territory westward, acted swiftly to initiate a conflict with Mexico when his offers to purchase the western territories were refused. The resulting Mexican-

American War achieved Polk's goal and at war's end, America's western border reached the Pacific Ocean.

But the surge of immigrants pressing westward would have forced the issue of American expansion. America, founded on principles that welcomed immigrants to the new land, was not kind to the inhabitants already living there.

Whole populations of Native Americans across the continent were either killed or displaced as settlers moved into their territories. The Mexican citizens of Alta California would have fared no better. And, when gold was discovered in California in 1849, there would have been no stopping the flood of humanity that poured into its borders.

Most Americans see the Mexican-American War as a footnote in history. But its impact was far greater than that; it changed the direction of the two countries forever.

ACKNOWLEDGEMENTS

As anyone who aspires to be an author knows, it is so important to have readers look at your words and point out the discrepancies, typos, repetitions and flaws. I have been particularly lucky to have friends carry out those tasks for me who have provided great guidance in making the book more readable and understandable.

I give great thanks to Sheri Henderson, Ruth McDonald, Dave Richards, Amber Greene and Matt West, who all took the time to read the book and offer their thoughts, criticisms and suggestions.

I particularly want to thank my son Allen Moody for encouraging me to pursue publishing this book for a larger audience than just our shared grandson (my great grandson) Loki Holmes.

Special thanks go to my publisher, Patricia Ross of Hugo House Publishers, Ltd., who expressed great enthusiasm and encouragement when I proposed the book to her. Her professional guidance and constructive additions to the book have vastly improved its appeal to all readers. And, last, but not least, I am so grateful for the wonderful design work of Ronda Taylor, HeartWork Publishing, who has created the final product for the reader.

ABOUT THE AUTHOR

Sandra Zink is a retired scientist. After receiving her doctorate in physics from the University of New Mexico, she worked as a medical physicist at two national laboratories: Los Alamos, New Mexico, and Berkeley, California. Her work there and at the National Cancer Institute, Bethesda, Maryland, involved the radiotherapy treatment of cancer patients using charged particles. Retired in 2001, she now lives in Loveland, Colorado.

INDEX

INDEX OF MAPS & ILLUSTRATIONS

www.ingramcontent.com/pod-product-compliance
Lightning Source LLC
Chambersburg PA
CBHW072147090426
42739CB00013B/3305